GEORGE B

pika-don

A TRUE STORY

George Bishop

Fisher Miller
PUBLISHING

First published 1995

Published by Fisher Miller Publishing,
Wits End, 11 Ramsholt Close,
North Waltham, Basingstoke,
Hants RG25 2DG, United Kingdom.

Printed by Turnergraphic, Winchester Road, Basingstoke.

ISBN 1-899077-02 2

A catalogue record for this book is available from the British Library

Acknowledgements

The author and publishers wish to thank the following for permission to quote from copyright material:

The Institute of Jesuit Sources for extracts from *One Jesuit's Spiritual Journey* by Pedro Arrupe, SJ (1986)

The Liturgical Press for extracts from 'Surviving the Atom Bomb' in *Recollections and Reflections of Pedro Arrupe, SJ* published by Michael Glazier Inc. (1986)

Cover artwork by Michael Steel

Maps drawn by Jon Beck

CONTENTS

PREFACE

I remember my surprise at reading that some people who had been directly under the atom bomb when it fell on Hiroshima in August 1945 had somehow miraculously survived. The survivors included a group of Jesuit priests led by Pedro Arrupe, later head of the whole Jesuit Order, and a pretty young woman, Miss Toshika Sasaki, who was permanently disfigured by the bomb, and very bitter about it. Later, when I read the life of Group-Captain Leonard Cheshire, VC, I learnt that he had been involved (as an observer) in the atomic attack on Nagasaki. Vanquished and victors, from both sides came 'men - and women – for others', their lives painfully sculpted forever by the horrors of the atomic holocaust, but their hearts open to the needs of those around them. Here was a story to tell. *Pika-Don* is that story.

George Bishop
Bourne
Lincolnshire
May 1995

part one

Prelude to Pika-Don

Chapter One

You are a Western Spy'

Hiroshima 1942

Pedro Arrupe entered his office. For a Rector's office, 'spartan' was too lavish a word for it: a desk, two chairs, a *tatami* (straw) mat on the floor, four bare white walls. He sat down.

Running footsteps thudded on the highly polished wood floor. A breathless, stocky figure stood in the doorway. It was Mr Kim. Tobias Kim was a Korean novice, studying for the priesthood.

'Father! The *Kempetai* are here,' he managed to blurt out.

The *Kempetai* were the all-powerful Japanese military secret police, expert in all manner of torture, who could extract any secret from the most obstinate of persons.

Father Arrupe went out to greet his visitors. In the corridor he met them: a man in jack-boots, and holding the hilt of his Samurai sword in his left hand, confronted him.

'Pedro Arrupe?' he inquired.

'Yes,' the Spanish priest nodded.

'Come with us. You are under arrest.'

'Arrest?' Father Arrupe repeated. 'What for?'

'You are a spy.'

The priest laughed at the very suggestion.

A crisp back-hand across his face from one of the soldiers sent him reeling.

'*Keto!* [hairy barbarian]. Do not be rude to your superior,' the soldier shouted.

Mr Kim, who had been standing back a respectful distance behind his Novice Master, rushed up to the guard.

'How dare you,' he shouted, his arm raised.

A rifle butt in the crutch of the young Korean sent him sprawling, doubled up in agony. There was little love between the Japanese and the Koreans.

The Captain came and stood over him.

'You keep out of this. Or you, too, will be under arrest.'

He returned to face Arrupe. Arrupe had by now realized the seriousness of the proceedings. This was no joking charade.

'You are a spy and a saboteur. You have been undermining the war effort.'

The Spanish priest was flabbergasted.

'Spy! Saboteur! Sabotage! What sabotage?'

'You have been preaching *heiwa* [peace] to your students.'

That was true. Father Arrupe had never lost an opportunity of denouncing war, of advocating peace.

'Of course I have been preaching *heiwa*,' he admitted.

'Don't you know there is a war on?' the officer shouted, now looking for all the world like an angry Fu Man Chu.

He glowered at the diminutive figure before him.

'Yes, sometimes war can be justified,' the priest countered. 'In self-defence for example.'

'That's right. We are defending ourselves against the British and American capitalists.'

'But it was you who attacked the Americans in Pearl Harbour. Not the other way round.'

There was a pause as the officer rehearsed his next line of argument.

'We are fighting for justice,' the officer continued, shaking the hilt of his sword for added emphasis. He went on, 'We are fighting to liberate Asia from the Western capitalists like Britain and the United States. We are fighting to return Asia to the Asian peoples. This is our duty.' The man was obviously completely convinced of the rightness of his cause.

The Secret Police officer was not going to degrade himself before his men any longer by debating on the morality of war in the passage way with a *gaijin* – a foreigner.

'Come with me. You are under arrest. You have just proved your guilt by speaking up for peace. We cannot have Western foreigners poisoning the minds of our brave young people with talk of peace.'

They began to take Father Arrupe away.

'Can I just get some things?' the priest asked.

'No – you cannot,' was the stern, emphatic response.

'Can I at least get my Breviary?'

'Breviary? What's that?'

'I need it for my Office,' Father Arrupe explained.

The man's eyes lit up.

'Office, office! That's it!'

Immediately the Secret Police captain ordered his men to search the office; that was where any incriminating letters and files would be hidden.

Before Father Arrupe could explain that his Office meant the daily prayers he was obliged to recite, he was unceremoniously bundled into a waiting truck and driven off. His colleagues and students, aroused by the shouting and general commotion, looked on in disbelief.

The truck wound its way down the valley. Hiroshima was surrounded by pine-wooded hills. The occupants of the truck lurched from side to side as the vehicle bumped its way over the dirt track, leaving behind a trail of yellow dust. The truck slowed as it passed through the village of Nagatsuka. Little knots of curious bystanders stared at the unusual sight of a *gaijin* being taken off in police custody. It was nearing the cold season. There was not so much activity on the terraced hill-sides, normally alive with peasants working in the rice fields. The valley was dotted with the single-storey houses of farmers, thatched with *susuki*, a kind of pampas grass.

The entrance to Ohshiba Park was still flanked by tall pines to guard it from evil spirits that would get entangled in the pine needles. The magnolias and wisteria were no longer in bloom. Arrupe would sometimes stroll in the Park, over the meticulously raked gravel representing the sea, dotted with the occasional boulder to represent an island. Near the tea house, shaped like a pagoda and surrounded by hostas and yakushimanum rhododendrons, clear water tumbled over a miniature waterfall and under tiny hump-back bridges built in zig-zag fashion to thwart the devil who could only travel in straight lines. He wondered if he would ever enjoy such walks again.

They went past Misasa, then over the River Ohta by the Misasi Bridge. The large Asano Park came into view. To the right rose up the massive walls of Hiroshima Castle, the flag of the rising sun fluttering from its *tenshu* tower, in the shape of a pagoda. He expected the truck to stop there. That was where he thought he would be incarcerated. The truck moved on. From the East Parade Ground he could hear the drill sergeants barking out orders to young recruits.

Most of the houses were single-storey buildings constructed of wood and paper. Occasionally a more modern building of steel and concrete, such as the Fukuyama Department Store or the Museum of Science and Industry, broke up the landscape of low houses. Far in the distance, in Hiroshima Bay, black smoke rose from the troop transports anchored in the port of Ujina. They were filling their holds with men and equipment for the far-flung Japanese Empire, now covering the entire Far East, embracing the Philippines, the Dutch East Indies, Malaysia, Indonesia, New Guinea, most of the Pacific Islands, Burma and extending right up to the gate of India at Kohima. Smoke from the Mitsubishi and other factories on the city's peripheries vied with the troop transports in polluting the atmosphere.

The number of vehicles increased as they neared the centre of the huge city; bursting streetcars clanged along the steel lines, passengers clinging seemingly to every piece of tram that offered a hand hold. And cyclists and pedestrians - there seemed to be millions of them. He recognised the familiar Mission House at Nobori-cho, where the Jesuits had their Church and School. Then through the suburb of Koi.

The truck finally stopped at Yamaguchi Prison. He knew Yamaguchi. That was his first parish. He was surprised to find a group of men and women at the prison gate. They were some of his former parishioners. News had travelled fast from Nagatsuka to Yamaguchi. He was pleased to see them again, but sad at the circumstances. They stood silent, disbelieving. Some women had their hands to their mouths. In the front stood the elderly John, his head bowed, holding his flat cap in his hand, like the peasant in Millet's famous painting *The Angelus*. John used to serve at his Masses.

Without any ceremony or consideration, Father Arrupe was bundled out of the truck and led through the gates, like some common felon. He was given rough prison uniform to wear – coarse black trousers and a grey, striped shirt. He was shoved into a cell. He heard the door clang behind him. He couldn't see a thing. It was pitch black. After some time he was able to make out the confines of his cell. There was no chair or table. Just a dirty straw mat on the hard stone floor, a metal receptacle in the corner. No window; very little light or air.

So began his solitary confinement. The cell door clanged open just once a day, when a warder passed him a bowl containing some rice. The warder never spoke. It was obvious he regarded the *gaijin* with contempt and hatred. In Japan Christianity was regarded as very un-Japanese, as against the *kokutai*, the national polity.

Father Arrupe was a Jesuit priest. The presence of the Jesuits in Japan went back four hundred years, to the time when Saint Francis Xavier first arrived in the country in 1549. At the beginning of the twentieth century they founded Sophia University in Tokyo. In 1933 a Novitiate was added to the University. In 1936 the Novitiate was moved to Hiroshima. In 1939 three young men entered as novices: the Japanese scholastic Matsumora (whose story is told later in this book), the Korean Kim and a Japanese Yokota who entered as a Brother.

As a student Arrupe had asked to be sent abroad to the foreign missions. The answer was always the same: wait. His Superiors were testing his vocation. Eventually in 1938 his wishes were met and he was sent to Japan. He was first sent to Ube, twenty-one hours by train from Tokyo, to serve his apprenticeship with some German priests. He was then appointed parish priest at Yamaguchi. In March 1942 he was appointed Novice Master and Rector of the Novitiate at Nagatsuka.

≤∫ℓ

Some days later Father Arrupe was taken out of his cell to be interrogated. He had to shield his eyes from the light. The spare, middle-aged Jesuit, his hair beginning to recede from his high forehead, stood before a bespectacled officer with a long Mongoloid face and goatee beard. He asked for a cup of water. All he got was an icy stare.

'Where were you born?'
'In Spain.'
'When?'
'In 1907.'
'What did you do in Spain?'
'I was a medical student.'
'Where?'
'At the University of Madrid.'
'Why did you leave?'
'To become a priest.'
'Why did you go to America?'
'To complete my studies.'
'But you could have completed your studies in Europe.... You went to America to become a spy?'

Father Arrupe shook his head at such a ridiculous suggestion. The cross-examination continued. Father Arrupe went on.

He was ordained in Holland in 1936. He then went to the United States to continue his studies. The interrogator wanted more details. From 1936 to 1937 at St. Mary's College, Kansas and from 1937 to 1938 in Cleveland, Ohio. A scribe noted down the dates and places carefully. And then, in October 1938, he came to Japan.

'Japan. Why to Japan?'
'I wanted to work here.'
'Or did the capitalist Americans send you here to spy?'

Again Arrupe shook his head. There were several more of these interrogations. At least he got some light and air whenever he was taken for questioning. Over and over he told them the same story: that he was born in Bilbao, the only boy of five children. His father was an architect, and newspaper publisher. His family were not wealthy, but they were not poor. His mother died when he was ten. His father died while he was a student at the university. He was then eighteen. After an unusual event at Lourdes he joined the Society of Jesus.

'What unusual event?'

'I saw three miracles happen.'

'Miracles!' the interrogator sneered, as he turned to his two equally disdainful companions. 'Tell us more,' he demanded.

Father Arrupe told them about the miracles. Then he continued. 'I was expelled from Spain in 1932, with all the other Jesuits.'

'Expelled! Why?'

'The Spanish Government was Communist. They were persecuting the Church.'

Perhaps his interrogators were glad to hear that. The Japanese were no lovers of Communism.

It was December and bitterly cold in the cell. He almost literally froze on his bare mat. He passed the days and nights, alone, in solitary confinement. He never knew if, when the heavy cell door opened again, it was not to take him out to be executed. Later he spoke of his grim experience in Yamaguchi prison as the most instructive time of his entire life: he learnt the science of silence, of severe and austere poverty, and of inner dialogue with his Maker. He had nothing but his thoughts as companions. He would think back to his family – his devout mother and father, his sisters. His days at the university. His love of opera.

I liked the theatre, music and the opera very much. Ah, the opera! We were the cheering section, and we would go to buy our tickets at a bar where the plates were made of metal and the silverware was attached to the tables by little chains; you see the kind of place it was. We were young then.

At that time Miguel Fleta was making his debut. He had been a vegetable seller, leading his donkey through the streets of Zaragosa, and he used to shout out his wares enthusiastically. As an opera singer he had a very powerful voice, but not yet very well trained. In Madrid he was a great success, and he was often interrupted by the enthusiasm of his admirers. He would beg the public on his knees to allow him to continue; and our group, we would applaud and cheer him even more. *

His mind often went back to other prison days – not as an inmate,

---

* Arrupe, P., *One Jesuit's Spiritual Journey*, the Insitute of Jesuit Sources, St Louis, Missouri, 1986, p.18.

but as a visitor. Before leaving the United States for Japan, while doing his tertianship in Cleveland, he would visit Spanish-speaking prisoners in a New York prison. The guards feared for his life as they saw someone wearing a dog-collar entering the cells of hardened criminals. Yet, after some months, when he told them he was leaving for Japan, these men, perpetrators of heinous acts, gave a party and sing-song in his honour.

He wondered how long he would be a prisoner. As long as some of those? Some had literally grown old in their narrow cells. Or would it be a short stay, like those who went to the electric chair? He wondered which of the two was better. He remembered young Jorge, to whom he had repeat the words once spoken to the repentant thief nearly two thousand years earlier, '*Esta noche vd ser conmigo en paraiso*' ('This day thou shalt be with Me in paradise'), as he was led away to the 'chair'.

How he longed for a visitor as the long days and nights merged into one another. But no one ever came. He saw no one, he spoke to no one. Solitary confinement meant just that.

Chapter Two

The Manhattan Project

Making the Atom Bomb, 1942–5

Just before the outbreak of World War II scientists discovered that if the nucleus of an uranium atom was bombarded by neutral atomic particles, called neutrons, the uranium atom could be split into two. This phenomenon was called nuclear fission. This fission was accompanied by release of more neutrons and of a tremendous amount of energy. If the new neutrons released were further used to split the nuclei of other uranium atoms the process could build up into a chain reaction, giving out vast amounts of energy. Could this energy be used in a bomb?

Early in 1940 confidential information was received that work on uranium fission was progressing in the Third Reich. The export of uranium ore was forbidden from the Joachimsthal mines in Czechoslovakia, Europe's foremost source of uranium, which had just been occupied by Hitler's Panzer divisions. Albert Einstein and Leo Szilard warned the American government of the dangers threatening all humanity if the Nazis were the first to make a nuclear bomb. It is to the credit of German scientists such as Otto Hahn and Walter Heisenberg that they sought to divert the attention of Hitler's war machine away from making such a bomb.

The US military authorities were very conservative. There was widespread mistrust of 'those fools, the long-haired guys', that is, the atomic scientists. In March 1940 Einstein sent a second letter to the President drawing attention to the intensification of German interest in uranium since the beginning of the war. Still nothing was done. At last, on 6 December 1941, just one day before the Japanese attack on Pearl Harbour and America's official entry into the war, the long-delayed decision was taken to invest substantial financial and technical resources to the construction of an atom bomb.

In August 1942 the United States Army was given the responsibility of organizing the efforts of American and British scientists to seek a way to harness nuclear energy for military purposes, an effort which became known as the Manhattan Project. In September 1942 General Groves, known as 'Greasy Groves' at West Point and hence nick-named 'Gee-Gee', was entrusted with the administration of this project. He was a big man, with an expanding waistline, addicted to munching chocolates. He was aggressive and blunt. He needed to be. Groves was chosen because he had more experience of supervising building construction than any other officer in the army.

In July 1943 J. Robert Oppenheimer was appointed to establish and administer a laboratory to carry out this assignment, to construct the mightiest weapon of all time. He was then 40 years old, a man of exceptional intelligence and clear-sightedness, who could quote Dante and Proust as easily as the latest developments in 'FF' ('fast fission'), a man aflame with inward passion, a man of irresistible personal magnetism – 'intellectual sex appeal' as it was called.

Oppenheimer was educated at the Los Alamos Ranch School for Boys, high up on the flat table-land or *mesa* that formed part of the 7300 feet Pajarito Plateau of the Jerez Mountains, among glistening peaks, scented pine-woods, sun-bathed glades, and striated canyons where the Red Indians had hunted. He chose this plateau of Los Alamos, near Santa Fe, New Mexico – the former seat of the Spanish viceroys who had ruled Mexico for centuries – with its savage beauty, aglitter with mesquite and yellow cactus, as the site for the Manhattan Project.

He had graduated with distinction under Max Born, the renowned theoretical physicist, in Gottingen in 1927. He then worked with Ernest O. Lawrence, the inventor of the cyclotron, at the Radiation Laboratory at Berkeley, University of California. The two were experimenting with an electromagnetic method of separating uranium 235, in which an atomic reaction is possible, and uranium 238, which is not susceptible to fission. In 1939 Niels Bohr had predicted that fission by slow neutrons would occur only in U_{235}. Although U_{235} and U_{238} are chemically identical elements, they have different masses. For instance, U_{238} has 238 protons and neutrons in its nucleus, whereas U_{235} has 235. Such elements are called isotopes. But uranium, as found in nature, is made up of U_{238} and U_{235} in proportions of 140 parts to one. A lot of uranium has to be obtained to get just one part of the fissionable U_{235}. Thus a vast amount of money would need to be spent, and a vast array of technologists employed, to produce enough U_{235} to make a bomb. It would cost \$20 million to produce less than 100 lbs of fissionable material.

In order to separate out the two isotopes an electric charge was given to the uranium atoms, which were then drawn into the field of a very powerful electromagnet. The atoms move in curving orbits, but because they have different masses, the isotopes move in slightly differing paths and can thus be collected in separate collectors. It was a slow process, but it worked.

However, the brilliant Italian scientist Enrico Fermi, a refugee from the Fascism then rampant in Europe, discovered another way of producing an atom bomb. If U_{235} was bombarded with neutrons a chain reaction occurred in which not only U_{238} was formed but also a new element, plutonium (Pu_{239}), together with more neutrons. Plutonium behaved like U_{235} in being fissionable and, moreover, it could be produced readily from the more common U_{238}. In 1942 the powers 'in the know' received a telegram which said 'The Italian navigator has landed.' This meant that Fermi had constructed the first nuclear power generator, in, of all places, the disused squash courts of the University of Chicago. He had been able to produce a slowed-down nuclear fission, a controlled chain reaction. But if this chain reaction was not controlled the tremendous energy released by fission could be used for mass destructive purposes, as in an atomic bomb.*

There were no factories for the production of the U_{235} or Pu_{239} which were needed for a nuclear chain reaction. Everything started from scratch. And everything was top-secret. In the spring of 1943 highly unusual 'tourists' began to drift into the sleepy city of Santa Fe. From there the 'tourists' would be taken to site Y, thirty-five miles away, and housed in white stucco buildings of Spanish type, with picturesque courtyards and wrought-iron gates, or lodged in 'guest ranches'. These 'tourists' were never referred to as 'Doctor' or 'Professor' – the sudden arrival of so many academics would have raised suspicions. One only spoke of the 'ph...s' (it was forbidden to mention their profession as physicists). Their address was US Army Post Box 1663.

The Army Pioneer Corps proceeded apace with erecting residential barracks and other buildings on the *mesa*. The once barren flatlands were transformed into a maze of roads, with temporary shelters and a network of telephone wires. Depending on the weather the roads would be dusty or seas of mud.

Oppenheimer would be up at daybreak. Sun-burned, in blue jeans with a silver studded belt and a garishly checked shirt, he would talk with everybody, his head tilted slightly to one side, coughing slightly and pausing significantly between sentences, his left hand in front of his lips as he spoke, a cigarette almost perpetually in his right hand. He even knew the labourers by their first names and they would gladly have given their lives for 'Señor' Opp.

---

* Fascinated by the idea of an almost continuous source of power, Fermi suggested to the US navy the idea of an atomic-powered submarine. The idea was thrown out as 'science fiction', but nevertheless in 1962 the world's first atomic submarine, the *Nautilus*, was launched.

Great secrecy was the order of the day. The more prominent of the atomic scientists had official bodyguards who followed them everywhere. Neils Bohr, for one, found this most irksome. At the time the Russians were trying hard to get any information about an atomic bomb. Though never a communist himself, Oppenheimer had associated with some in the past and so he, too, was under close scrutiny. Out of a total of 150 000 people who were eventually employed on the Manhattan Project barely a dozen were allowed an overall view of the plan. Very few knew they were working on an atomic bomb at all. The people working in the computer centre at Los Alamos had no idea of the real purpose behind the complicated calculations they carried out.

Meanwhile a letter informed General Groves that a first atomic bomb had to be ready for testing by mid-July 1944 and a second bomb had to be available for war purposes by August 1945. But there were still huge questions to be answered and huge problems to be surmounted. In 1939 F. Perrin had shown that there is a minimum amount of U_{235} required before a chain reaction can begin. This minimum quantity is called the 'critical mass'. With smaller quantities, with relatively high proportions of surface area, too many neutrons are lost to the atmosphere for the chain reaction to begin. But what was this critical mass? And how was anyone to find it without being caught themselves in the middle of a catastrophic nuclear chain reaction? There was every danger of premature experiments leading to a premature explosion.

The principle behind the atomic bomb was to have two parts of U_{235}, each below the critical mass – whatever that was – and keep them apart. Then, once over the bombing target, one of these two pieces would be shot into the other piece, thus making the total mass greater than the critical mass – or 'crit' as it was called in Los Alamos jargon. A chain reaction would occur, resulting in an enormous explosion, and at the same time producing intense heat and radioactive rays capable of destroying the cells of the human body.

Otto Frisch, the discoverer of nuclear fission, had been brought to Los Alamos from England, specifically to work on the problem of critical mass. Working under him was a skinny young Canadian, Louis Slotin, born of Russian parents who had fled their country when Stalin's pogroms began. The quantity of uranium required, the scattering angle and the range of neutrons to be emitted by the chain reaction, the speed at which the two parts would have to collide and answers to a whole series of other questions could be estimated approximately. But absolute precision and certainty could only be attained by way of experimental trial and error.

Slotin would experiment away without taking any special protective measures. All his life he had gone in search of adventure and excitement. As a young man he had volunteered for service in the Spanish Civil War. He joined the RAF and flew on active missions until it was discovered that at his medical examination he had concealed the fact that he was near-sighted.

His only experimental instruments were two screw-drivers by means of which he allowed two hemispheres containing uranium to slide towards one another on a rod. He would monitor the increasing radioactivity as the two hemispheres approached each other. His object was to just reach the critical point, the very first step in the chain reaction, which would immediately stop the instant he parted the hemispheres again. If he let this point pass, or was not quick enough in breaking the proximity of the hemispheres, the total mass of uranium would be super-critical and he would be right in the middle of a nuclear explosion. By this method he discovered that the critical mass for a chain reaction to take place in U_{235} was 1.5 kg.

Slotin knew, of course, that he was dicing with death or 'twisting the dragon's tail' as he put it. Frisch had already nearly lost his life during one of these experiments. Slotin was not so lucky. On 21 May 1946 he was again experimenting on the critical mass for an atomic bomb test which was to be carried out in the waters surrounding the South Sea atoll of Bikini. Suddenly his screw-driver slipped and the two hemispheres of uranium rolled towards one another.

'Take cover,' he screamed to his colleagues, among them the Englishman Klaus Fuchs. By now the two hemispheres had passed the 'crit' point. The whole room was instantly filled with a dazzling, bluish glare. His seven colleagues made a dash for it. Slotin, brave man that he was, grabbed the two hemispheres with his bare hands and pulled them apart, thus interrupting the chain reaction which would have caused a nuclear explosion. Had he ducked he could have saved himself from the full effect of the radiation.

By now the neutron count had risen so high that the delicate instrument could no longer register the intense radiation. Slotin realized at once that he was bound to succumb to the effects of the massive radiation dose which he had absorbed. But he did not lose control of himself for a moment. He could still make some vital measurements. He told his colleagues to stand exactly where they had been at the instant of the disaster. On the blackboard he drew a sketch of their relative positions so that doctors could measure the amount of radiation to which each of those present had been exposed.

Nine days later the man who had experimentally determined the critical mass for the first atom bomb died in terrible agony. He was not the first man to die in the race to develop the bomb. On 21 August 1945, during an experiment with a small quantity of fissile material, Henry Dagnian set off a chain reaction for the fraction of a second. His right hand received a huge dose of radiation. After admission to hospital within half an hour of the accident, he noticed at first only a certain loss of sensation in the fingers, occasionally superseded by slight tingling. But soon his hands grew more and more swollen and his general condition deteriorated rapidly. Delirium set in. The young physicist complained of severe internal pains, for it was now that the effect of the gamma rays, which had penetrated far beneath the skin to the interior of the body, began to be perceptible. His hair dropped out. The white corpuscles of his blood increased rapidly. Twenty-four days later he died.

There were two methods of making the bomb. In the 'gun-type' bomb a small sub-critical mass of U_{235} was fired into a larger, also sub-critical mass, and so set off a nuclear explosion. Alternatively the explosion could be induced by 'implosion', where the fissionable material would go off inwardly rather than outwardly. A blast of conventional high explosive is directed inward towards a mass of plutonium, squeezing together the central core (about the size of a cricket ball) until it becomes critical and detonates into a ball of fire equivalent to twenty-thousand tons of TNT. No one knew for sure which kind of bomb would function better – if, indeed, either would work at all. Groves ordered both types to be built simultaneously.

Some days before the first test of the bomb it was an open secret in Alamogordo, even among the wives and children of the Los Alamos scientists, that something very important and special was being prepared. The test was referred to under the code name 'Trinity'. The reason for this blasphemous name was because at the time the first three atom bombs to be made were nearing completion.

But would the 'gadgets' really go off? Luis Alvarez, who developed the trigger of the bomb, often told over-confident colleagues how in 1943, when his invention for blind landing of aircraft had been demonstrated to the military authorities it had failed no less than four times before it finally worked. The scientists even had a betting pool whether the first atomic bomb would be a 'girl' (a dud) or a 'boy' (a success). They also bet on the size of the explosion, if any.

On Thursday 12 July and Friday 13 July the components of the interior explosive mechanism of the test bomb were taken from Los Alamos by the 'back door', along a secret road, to the test area, known as *Journada del Muerto* (Death Tract) at Alamogordo Air Base, in New Mexico. Here in the middle of the desert, a tall, 100-foot high, iron scaffolding had been erected to hold the bomb on a wooden platform at the top. In order to diminish the amount of dust that would be sucked up into the fireball and fed back to the earth as radioactive fall-out, it was decided to detonate the bomb from a high tower. It was also necessary that there should be no rain, with wind blowing in the right direction, so that any radioactive fall-out would be carried into the empty desert.

For weeks and weeks not a drop of rain had fallen. A hot, dry wind blew from the New Mexico desert. The grass withered, the foliage and pine needles on the trees dried up. Forest fires broke out here and there, sometimes too close to the town of laboratories, all constructed of timber. But now the weather changed. The skies darkened and lightning flickered in the distance over the Sangre de Cristo Mountains. Because of the danger of thunderstorms it was decided not to put the test bomb in position until the last possible moment. A bomb of about equal size, filled with ordinary explosive, was hung up on the scaffolding to test the conditions. That night it was struck by lightning and went off with a huge bang.

The final assembly of the bomb began in a nearby ranch-house the next morning. The core of the bomb consisted of two close-fitting hemispheres of plutonium. As the two hemispheres were nursed to where they were almost critical, tension mounted in the room. Outside, four jeeps, with motors idling, stood by for a quick departure should an accidental chain reaction be triggered. Periodically Oppenheimer entered the room to watch proceedings, but he was so nervous he was asked to leave until the assembly was completed. The pieces were machine-tooled to the finest measurements. The two joined hemispheres took the form of a globe, which the scientists called a plug. The men in the ranch-house raised the plug to the top of the metal tower where the explosives men waited anxiously. The plug was then lowered by a manually operated hoist into the explosives assembly. The men, perspiration covering their faces, began manoeuvring the plug into position. They knew that the material was so near to being critical that the slightest jar would set off an explosion.

Then came calamity. The plug would not move further. It was jammed tightly. The intense heat of the day had caused the plug to expand; it would not enter the cooler explosives assembly. Word went out on the field telephones that there was a technical hitch. Dr Robert Bacher, head of the Bomb Physics Division at Los Alamos, reassured the group that time would solve the problem. In three minutes' time, the insertion of the plug was completed.

The test was scheduled to take place at four a.m. on 16 July 1945.

By two o'clock in the grey pre-dawn scientists and GIs taking part in the test were assembled in the Base Camp, ten miles from Point Zero. They put on their dark glasses and smeared their faces with anti-sunburn lotion against the ultra-violet rays. The loudspeakers played dance music. The music was interrupted to say that bad weather rendered a postponement necessary. After consultation with the meteorological experts it was finally decided to detonate the bomb at 5.30 a.m.

Seated in front of the firing console in a bunker was Joe McKibbern. The instruments told him that everything was functioning according to plan and on schedule. He lifted the cover to expose the automatic timer which would activate all the firing and timing circuits at the top of the tower in the final minute. To his right sat Joe Hornig, eyes glued to the panel and gripping tightly the 'stop' switch which he would throw if anything went wrong.

At 5.10 a.m. Oppenheimer's deputy, Saul Allison, began to send out time signals. General Groves, at Base Camp, was reminding everybody to have on their sunglasses and lie down on their faces with their heads turned away. Anyone trying to observe the fireball with the naked eye would be blinded.

During the waiting, which seemed an eternity, hardly a word was spoken. Would the two years of toil and $5 billion cost be justified? they wondered. Would the explosion, if it happened, set off a global reaction that would destroy the world? General Groves wondered if he had taken every possible step to ensure rapid evacuation in the case of disaster, such as widespread radioactive fall-out. He had been given authorization to declare martial law if necessary. All air traffic between El Paso and Albuquerque had been re-routed or suspended on the day of the test. An even bigger worry was what he would do if after the count-down nothing happened. This was history's greatest gamble. Never before had so much time, money and effort been lavished on anything, for peace or war, that was completely untested, unproven and, indeed, unprovable. It was not possible to test such a nuclear explosion until more than $20 million had been spent on employing half a million people and constructing three complete cities in remote areas of the American wilderness.

At zero hour minus five minutes a short siren shrilled through the darkness before a possible man-made dawn. A green Verey signal gave the final warning. At zero minus forty-five seconds McKibbern started the automatic timer. Circuits were triggered in swift succession. Only Hornig, his knuckles white with gripping the 'stop' switch, could now prevent events proceeding to a conclusion.

'Zero!'

At 5.34 a.m. man pre-empted nature's sunrise.

A soaring brilliance rent the darkness. The desert went ghost white. The *mesa* bleached out. A huge, swirling ball of fire, getting bigger and bigger, climbed steadily higher. Carson Mark, one of the senior officers, thought the ball of fire would not stop growing until it had consumed all heaven and earth.

'Good God!' he shouted, 'I believe the long-haired boys have lost control.'

Only man's primordial discovery of fire could compare with this nuclear detonation.

There was absolute silence and this absence of sound was unnatural and frightening. Then, out of the fire, came a shock wave. The GIs watched in awe as the fireball rose steadily, blood red, blanketing the earth in an eerie, yellow-crimson, light. At 15 000 feet the top flattened out into a giant mushroom, attached to earth by an elongating stalk of radioactive dust. At 39 000 feet it took on a purple crown of ionized air that drifted north over the desert. Instruments showed that the explosion was equivalent to one of 20 000 tons of TNT. At its centre the temperature was four times that at the core of the sun; the radio-activity given off was one million times that of all the radium in the world. Nothing could have survived such a bomb. A huge hole was blasted in the crust of the earth.

General Farrell reported thus:

The whole country was lighted by a searing light with an intensity many times that of the midday sun ... Thirty seconds after the explosion came, first, the air blast pressing hard against the people and things, to be followed almost immediately by the strong, sustained awesome roar which warned of doomsday and made us feel that we puny things were blasphemous to dare tamper with the forces heretofore reserved to the Almighty. Words are inadequate tools for the job of acquainting those not present with the physical, mental, and psychological effects. It had to be witnessed to be realized.*

Even so cool and matter-of-fact a person as Enrico Fermi received a profound shock. Never before had he allowed anyone else to drive his car. But on this occasion he confessed that he did not feel capable of sitting at the wheel and asked a friend to take it for him on the road back to Los Alamos.

---

* Quoted in Robert Jungk, *Brighter than a Thousand Suns*, Penguin, 1958, p.184.

Delighted with the turn of events General Groves turned to Farrell and said: 'The war's over. One or two of those things, and Japan will be finished.'

In the event all the estimates of the burst were far too low. The nearest was that of a new-comer to the coterie of scientists. When asked how his estimate came to be reasonably close, he said he merely wanted to be polite to his older, experienced colleagues and so gave a figure that was flatteringly high. Even that 'flatteringly high' guess was far smaller than the real burst. The effect of the blast was twenty times greater than calculations had predicted. The bomb was no longer spoken of as a 'firecracker' but as a 'shattering experience'.

On the way back the buses were ordered not to stop at Albuquerque, two hours away, lest the people saw the obvious elation on the faces of those involved in the test. They were taken on to Los Alamos, another three hours away.

The general public was told nothing about the first world-shattering atomic bomb. Inhabitants near the test area up to a distance of 125 miles had seen an unusually bright light in the sky about 5.30 a.m. They were given false information that a munitions depot had blown up. But slowly word leaked out. A whispering campaign carried the news of the fireball, the mushroom cloud, the intense heat, to co-workers in the other Manhattan Project laboratories, such as at Oak Ridge. Some of them signed a petition urging that the atomic bomb should not be used against Japan without prior demonstration of its horrendous effects and without the opportunity to surrender.

In the summer of 1939 Leo Szilard had visited Einstein to get his assistance in persuading the American government to construct an atomic bomb as a preventive measure. Now he approached Einstein again to write to President Roosevelt urging him not to use the atomic bomb on Japan. The letter lay on the President's table, unopened, when he died on 12 April 1945. Several other scientists petitioned against the use of so awesome a weapon of mass destruction. E.O. Lawrence, Director of the Radiation Laboratory at Berkeley, University of California, was one of these. He probably objected at least partly because some of his best pupils had been Japanese. Two years earlier the Pope had issued a warning against the destructive use of atomic energy, in a speech to the Pontifical Academy of Sciences on 21 February, 1943, when the ordinary public still knew nothing about the atomic bomb.

The greatest irony was that the first atomic bomb used against Japan was not the kind tested in Alamogordo, but the other 'gun-barrel' type, which had never been tested at all.

Chapter Three

The Thin Man

Tinian, South Pacific, July-August 1945

'Halt or I fire.' The words boomed above the wind and rain of the sudden Pacific squall.

The man running across the coral, doubled up against the rain and holding on to his forage cap, stopped, now bolt upright as if bayoneted in the lower back. He didn't move. He heard boots crunching behind him. The guard came round and fixed the now rigid sprinter with a rifle at his throat.

'I was running because of the rain,' stammered the intruder, finally, gazing down at a gun barrel peeping out of a rain-soaked mackintosh.

'Sir,' the guard replied in a southern American drawl, 'we shoot to kill. Rain or shine,' he added with relished emphasis.

He looked carefully at the identification tag on the other man's khaki drill shirt pocket. He read every word on the card and finally handed it back to its owner.

'Pass, Sir,' he snapped.

Heaving a sigh of relief the man did just that, making sure to walk despite the pelting rain. He made for another barbed wire fence around a Quonset hut. Again he was stopped by a US marine, who not only scrutinized the identity tag very carefully but demanded the pass-word.

By now the squall had lessened in intensity and he could pick out the ocean breakers thudding against the white coral of the tiny island of Tinian, one of the Marianna group of islands in the vast Pacific Ocean.

Yet again he was stopped before he was allowed to enter the 'inner sanctum', accessible only to those with special 'need to know' passes.

The man lowered his head as he bowed under the flap of the camouflaged Quonset hut. He turned his back to the entrance to the hut, took off his cap and poured out a cataract of water that had gathered in the crown of his headgear to augment the rainwater that by now had formed a muddy moat round the building.

It took his eyes some time to get accustomed to the dark from the dazzling glare outside.

'Welcome! Sit down,' an unmistakably Californian voice came from a man doubled up over some equipment on a bare table. As he slowly straightened up, the visitor saw that he was an exceptionally tall man. He wiped his hands on a hand towel and came over to the newcomer.

'I'm Alvarez. Luis Alvarez,' the man clad in camouflaged overalls said, as he came over to join his visitor. They shook hands.

'So you're the famous Cheshire,' the physicist smiled as he greeted his guest.

'It's a privilege to meet you,' he went on.

Group Captain Leonard Cheshire, VC, DSO, DFC, sat down. In June 1940, as a nervous twenty-two year old, Cheshire had joined the RAF. By September of that year he was captain of an aircraft. The following month he received the first of his three DSOs for 'brilliant leadership and skill' during a raid over Cologne. In 1941 he was promoted to Squadron Leader. He did three operational tours over Germany. His next promotion to Group Captain put him behind a desk for six months. In July 1943 he voluntarily dropped rank in order to take command of 617 Squadron (the 'Dambusters'), the special-duties squadron formed to blow up the Mohne and Eder dams in the Ruhr. The raids undertaken by the squadron and led by him personally were demonstrations of incredible daring and courage which earned him the supreme award of the Victoria Cross in 1944.

One day in July 1945 Cheshire was at his office at the British Joint Staff Mission in Washington. His mission was to help plan Bomber Command's role in the forthcoming invasion of Japan, scheduled for 1 November of that year. He was busy with files detailing the problems the US Marines would meet in their frontal assaults on the enemy coast. The Marines had suffered huge casualties, not only during their sea-borne landings, but even long after it was clear to their Japanese opponents that all was lost. The Japanese had even more casualties, fighting with incredible tenacity and bravery. If this was how the Japanese fought on foreign shores how much tougher would the fighting be on their own homeland, where they had three million men under arms and huge stocks of ammunition and equipment. The nearest American foothold to Japan was the island of Okinawa, recently captured by the Americans with huge losses in men, 450 miles from Japan. Bomber Command would have to operate from one thousand miles away or even more.

Cheshire was ordered to report to Field Marshal Maitland Wilson, head of the British Joint Staff Mission. The Field Marshal told him that the Americans had built an atomic bomb, the first of which had been successfully detonated in a test the day before. Wilson explained that a determined effort was being made to persuade the Japanese to surrender, but if they refused the bomb would be dropped on a target in Japan in the hope of ending the war without the need of an invasion.

Britain had played a leading role in the early development of the atomic bomb, and Churchhill and Truman had agreed that two British observers would accompany the attack on Japan. William Penney, a physicist, who had been with the atom bomb project from the beginning was one observer. The other was to be an operational pilot. Who better to choose than Group Captain Cheshire? He was to learn all about the technical aspects of using such a weapon and report back to the Prime Minister.

He was told that he would be briefed by General Groves, who had been in charge of the atom bomb project in New Mexico, and who would arrange transport for him to the tiny Pacific island of Tinian. Here a special-duties squadron of B-29 Superfortress bombers was based. Cheshire was placed under a strict oath of secrecy and warned that he would be shadowed by security forces.

He and Penney were 'processed' through the principal gateway to the Pacific theatre of battle which was Hamilton Field, near San Francisco. On a C54, known as a Green Hornet, of Air Transport Command, with a seven-man crew they began the long two-and-half-day flight to Tinian, via Hawaii, Johnston Island, Kwajalein and Guam. At Guam they had breakfast with General Curtis Le May, Chief of Staff to the Commander-in-Chief Pacific Strategic Air Force.

On the drive from the airfield at Tinian, past flat, rolling, fields of sugar-cane, they passed a cemetery in which lay the bodies of 1100 Marines killed in the bitter fighting to capture this tiny piece of atoll rock one year earlier. They were shown to a simple tent which was their billet. There were two teams on Tinian – the scientists and the aircrew. The scientists, under Brigadier General Farrell, were charged with the technical aspects of the bomb, while the aircrew, commanded by Colonel Tibbetts, were responsible for delivering the bomb. The two teams were amalgamated into one unit – 509th Bombardment Group. This Group was secluded from the rest of the island, on the north shore, and guarded with unusually strict security. Anyone approaching the aircraft without identifying himself would be shot.

The greater part of the explosive heart of the atom bomb had been brought to Tinian in the heavy cruiser *Indianapolis*, the fastest in the American fleet, under great secrecy. Only three men on the vessel had any idea of what she was carrying. The rest simply supposed there must be something very important in the lead-lined bucket (containing the charges of precious enriched uranium 235) and the large fifteen-foot wooden crates (containing the firing gun and case for the bomb) which had been hoisted aboard on the morning of

16 July 1945, shortly before the cruiser put to sea. During the voyage from San Francisco to Tinian very special security measures were taken for defence against hostile submarines. The captain had strict orders to guard the mysterious cargo day and night and 'if the ship goes down, save the cargo at all costs, in a lifeboat if necessary.' Everyone heaved a sigh of relief when the top-secret cargo was off-loaded. The *Indianapolis* sailed off again. But at five minutes to midnight on 30 July the cruiser was torpedoed by the Japanese submarine I-516, only 316 of the crew of 1196 surviving the disaster.

The next day a Green Hornet, carrying as passengers only a colonel and a major who insisted on personally carrying a peculiar yellow box, landed at Tinian. What lay inside the yellow box was the nuclear core of the bomb.

ℒℛ

The man in the overalls pulled up a chair to face Cheshire. Alvarez had worked on the atomic bomb project at Los Alamos. In fact, it was he who had succeeded in constructing the complex release mechanism of the bomb, accurate to one millionth of a second. While at Tinian he had also developed a measuring device to be dropped at the same time as the bomb. It was designed to transmit radio signals to the bombing aircraft giving information on the strength of the shock waves released by the new weapon.

Cheshire shivered as he left the shimmering heat outside and entered the hut, air-conditioned against humidity and dust. He gazed around the walls of the Quonset. There seemed to be tools and odd bits of equipment and manuals and books of instructions lying all over the place. There was no sign of any bomb, but this 'inner sanctum' was where the work of assembling and loading the mechanism for detonating the bomb was supposed to be carried out.

'You're wondering where the bomb is?' Alvarez asked.

Cheshire nodded.

'That's it there,' Alvarez said as he walked across to a yellow box lying on the floor. 'We call it the "Thin Man",' he said as he casually kicked the lid open with his foot. Cheshire was taken aback at such liberties being taken with the world's ultimate weapon.

Cheshire walked across to the yellow box. Inside was a metallic sphere the size of a football. It didn't look much different from all the other bits and pieces of metal-ware lying round the hut.

He must have looked startled.

'Have no fear,' Alvarez reassured him. 'It's perfectly harmless – as it is!' he added with a smile. 'Here, touch it if you like. But you'll need gloves first.'

The Briton was reluctant to do so. But when Alvarez held out a pair of gloves he pulled them on, bent down and touched the sleeping giant as if it was some deadly hamadryad. 'The sensation,' Cheshire later reported, 'was like the first time you touch a snake; you recoil from what you know will feel slimy and repulsive and then, to your surprise, find it is warmish, almost friendly.'

'Why do you call it the "Thin Man"?' Cheshire asked.

'Oh,' replied Alvarez. 'We have a "Thin Man" and a "Fat Man". If the "Thin Man" doesn't work, we'll drop the "Fat Man".'

'Won't it work?' Cheshire asked, sensing some doubt entering into the conversation.

'I hope so,' Alvarez replied. 'That's my job – to see that it does work. A somewhat similar kind worked at Alamogorde on the first test. But that was in the comparative peace of the New Mexico desert. This will be different – very different – on a combat mission.'

He paused. Then he continued, 'The technical and logistical problems are enormous. Japan is well over one thousand miles away. The bombers must carry enough fuel for a round trip of 3000 miles. That's a great deal of weight to carry.'

'Yes,' Cheshire agreed. 'I have been watching the huge *Superfortresses* taking off.'

From Tinian the giant bombers launched daily raids with ordinary explosive and incendiary bombs on the mainland of Japan. The runway ended at a cliff edge and the heavily-laden B-29s would lumber painfully to the end, often dropping out of sight below the cliff.

'As I see them roll over the edge of the cliff,' Cheshire continued, 'I wonder if they will ever get airborne.'

'A few have crashed on take-off,' admitted Alvarez. 'And that wouldn't be nice with the Thin Man on board. Even after take-off the dangers are immense,' he continued. 'The plane carrying the bomb could be hit or shot down by enemy fighters. The *Mitsubishi Zero* is a good plane. Too fast and manoeuvrable for the Supers.' He paused for a while. 'And then everything would really go sky-high.'

He burst into a laugh. 'Including you,' still laughing and pointing at Cheshire. (He knew Cheshire would be accompanying the plane as an observer.)

Cheshire had faced enemy anti-aircraft fire many times. This would be a new experience and a new fear – being incinerated and vaporized by an awesome new weapon.

Arguments were raging as to whether or not the atomic bomb should be used against Japan. One side argued that Japan was already nearly finished. With the defeat of Germany in May 1945, a similar fate for Japan was inevitable. The Japanese no longer had enough food in stock and their fuel reserves were practically exhausted. Many in the country were ready to capitulate, and diplomatic feelers were being sent out in Sweden and elsewhere. Foreign Minister Togo had admitted that 'Japan is defeated. We must face and act accordingly.' The Emperor himself was in favour of peace initiatives.

But it was the military who were the power behind the Japanese throne. The Emperor was nothing but a manipulative front for the military authorities, the *Gumbutsu*. The Emperor's role was to reign not rule. From the very outset of their adventurism into Manchuria, China and then East Asia, the military had presented themselves as the natural leaders and liberators of the region from the British and American imperialists. The speed and comprehensiveness of their early military successes, and their astute propaganda, had led the people to look upon the armed forces as all-conquering and invincible.

In the first attack on the American fleet in Pearl Harbour in 1941, eight American ships were sunk, twelve damaged and 460 planes put out of service. On the second day of the war, the Japanese landed in the Philippines. On the nineteenth they occupied Hong Kong; shortly thereafter, British Borneo. In rapid succession, they over-ran South East Asia and prepared for an attack on India. Within two months, 914 Allied planes and 92 ships had been destroyed. There were 22370 prisoners of war, and the spoils of war included 200 tanks and 3650 automobiles in 307 raids. Within six months the number of ships sunk climbed to 360 and the campaign continued with the landing in New Guinea, the conquest of the Caroline Islands, and the preparations for an attack on Australia. The war had been so remote from Japan that it had made no impact on the ordinary person.

But Japan had over-reached her lines of communication and supply. Soon the mighty output of American war factories began to have their effect. The Japanese advance was gradually slowed, then halted and finally slowly rolled back to Japan. The Allies advanced across the Pacific in a series of gigantic steps, from island to island. The object of this grim island-hopping campaign was to capture bases from which US bombers could attack the Japanese homeland.

With the fall of Saipan, 1200 miles to the south of Japan, in November 1944, the mainland came within range of the new and revolutionary B-29 bomber. From the Marianas giant B-29 *Superfortresses* flew day after day in their thousands. Working to a systematic plan they burnt the hearts out of 66 major cities. Even so, the military dictatorship duped the people into believing that this

29

The Pacific War Zone

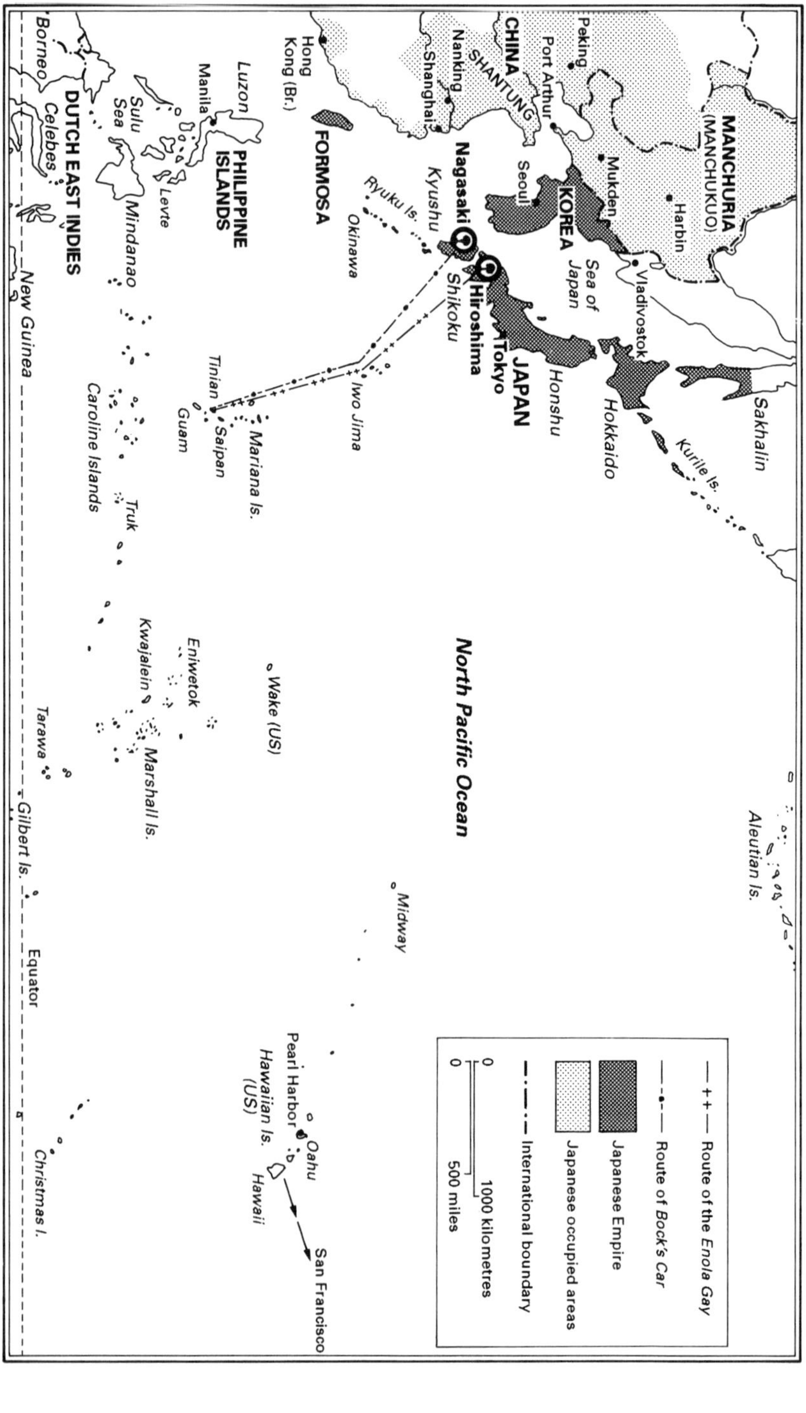

was only a necessary price for the victory that would ultimately be won. The losses of Pacific islands, they argued, were in reality defensive victories because of the high casualties inflicted on the Americans, and the closer the war came to Japan itself the more the advantage would swing in their favour. Final victory would be theirs and preservation of the national honour demanded nothing less than a fight to the last man. To the Gumbutsu surrender was unthinkable. Instead of capitulation the Supreme Command issued the following resolution:

With a faith born of eternal loyalty as our inspiration, we shall, thanks to the advantage of our terrain and the loyalty of our people, prosecute the war to the bitter end in order to uphold our national essence (*Kokutai*), protect the Imperial land and achieve our goals of conquest.

Because the Emperor remained *mokusatsu* (silent), it was assumed that he approved and plans for Operation Decision, the final decisive battle on the homeland, were put in hand. Right until the very end, the army continued to insist that it was here that victory would be wrested from apparent defeat 'even if it costs a million men'. Later this slogan was to become 'one hundred million men'.

In the face of this obstinacy what could the Americans do? Admirals Leahy and King believed victory could be won by air and sea power alone, by stepping up the already devastating bomber offensive against the mainland and by mounting a total sea blockade. When Admiral Leahy was told about the atom bomb he listened in disbelief, adding, 'the bomb will never go off.' General MacArthur, Supreme Allied Commander Pacific, however, disagreed with the two Admirals. He argued that aerial bombing was an unproved war-winning instrument, as the battle for Europe had shown, and that to occupy a ring of island bases round Japan, as the Admirals wanted, would disperse Allied forces even more than they already were. He went ahead with his plans for the invasion of Japan – Operation Olympic, the invasion of the southern island of Kyushu scheduled for 1 November – and for Operation Coronet, the assault against the central Tokyo plain, in March or April 1946.

With the first landing only four months away, training for Olympic had already begun on the southern beaches of Guam. Yet this was a step no one wanted if it could possibly be avoided. Ever since May the American public had been deeply affected by the staggering losses suffered by their forces. The battle over Okinawa lasted from 6 April to 21 June and cost the Americans 12 000 dead. The Japanese fought with incredible tenacity and fanaticism and total contempt of death. More Americans had been killed or severely wounded in the caves of Okinawa than during the whole campaign for the reconquest of the Philippines. If this was how the Bushido warriors fought for a relatively unimportant island, how would they fight on the mainland itself?

The Japanese tended to idealize death at the expense of life. In some mysterious way, the way a person died seemed to be almost more important than the way he lived. For a soldier total sacrifice was demanded. He would hold on to one bomb or grenade with which he could kill himself rather than surrender. A soldier who surrendered was dishonoured for the rest of his life and could never return to his native country. Hence the notorious Japanese contempt for prisoners of war.

It was clear that the Japanese would fight to the bitter end, until the last surviving Japanese soldier was dug out of a cave on top of Mount Fuji. By then more than half a million GIs would have lost their lives. No one wanted another Okinawa from one end of Japan to the other. MacArthur planned on a final assault team of 36 divisions, one and a half million men. Against this the Japanese had five million soldiers and five thousand *kamikaze* (suicide) aircraft to throw against the invading troops.

MacArthur estimated his campaign would last a year and cost a minimum of two million Japanese lives and one million American and Allied. The use of an atomic bomb would entail the sacrifice of possibly a quarter of a million Japanese lives. On the other hand, use of the weapon could prevent even greater destruction of life and property on *both* sides.

A further concern was that the defeat of Japan would not necessarily mean the surrender of their forces elsewhere. Burma, Malaya, Borneo, Java, Siam, and Indo-China were still occupied, under the command of Field Marshal Terauchi, an aristocrat and fanatical imperialist, who totally rejected any idea of a negotiated peace. He had made it very clear that his commanders were to resist to the end in the best Samurai tradition, and had issued written orders for the execution of all POWs the moment the Allied offensive for the recapture of South-East Asia opened. The start of the Allied offensive was set for 6 September. All POWs in Japan had been summoned and told that they would be shot or killed by flame-throwers as soon as the first American set foot on Japanese soil.

The alternative was the hope that the use of an atomic bomb, or if necessary two, would administer such a shock as to bring about a change of heart in the military and persuade them to surrender. There had been some suggestions that a demonstration of the power of the bomb should first be made. But this was ruled out as unrealistic.

On 1 June, after much soul-searching, the committee advising President Truman, who had just taken office in April, as the thirty-third President of the United States, unanimously recommended that an atomic bomb should be released on Japan as soon as possible.

To extract a genuine surrender from the Emperor and his military advisors, they must be administered a tremendous shock which would carry convincing proof of our power to destroy the Empire. Such a shock would save many times the number of lives, both American and Japanese, than it would cost.

The committee agreed they should first try to persuade Japan to surrender by warning her in the strongest possible way of the consequences if she did not.

In the last volume of his war memoirs Winston Churchill relates how on 4 July 1945, when he was at the Potsdam Conference with President Truman and Stalin, he was handed a sheet of paper with the cryptic message: 'Babies satisfactorily born'. This meant the experimental test of the atomic bomb the previous day had been successful.

We seemed suddenly to have become possessed of merciful abridgment of the slaughter in the East and of a far happier prospect in Europe. I have no doubt that these thoughts were present in the minds of my American friends. At any rate, there never was a moment's discussion as to whether the atomic bomb should be used or not. To avert a vast, indefinite butchery, to bring the war to an end, to give peace to the world, to lay healing hands upon its tortured peoples by a manifestation of overwhelming power at the cost of a few explosions, seemed, after all our toils and perils, a miracle of deliverance.*

On 27 July 1945 Allied leaders meeting at Potsdam broadcast a demand for the unconditional surrender of Japan. That evening, in the long canvas tent in Tinian which served as a Mess, Alvarez and Cheshire listened to the voice of President Truman, speaking over a crackling radio. 'We call upon the government of Japan to proclaim now the unconditional surrender of all Japanese armed forces ... ,' he said. 'The alternative for Japan is total and utter destruction.'

---

* Quoted in B.H. Liddell Hart, *History of the Second World War*, Cassell, London, 1970, p. 692.

Influential people such as Joseph Grew, the former US ambassador to Tokyo, warned the American government that unconditional surrender had little chance of acceptance by the Japanese for the simple reason that it did not recognize the sacred person of the Emperor. He was not a war criminal and, indeed, had tried to prevent the war from starting. Every Japanese would resist a surrender that could mean the Emperor might be tried as a war criminal, and they would never co-operate with an Occupation that sanctioned such a sacrilege. But arguments like these were rejected and the broadcast went ahead.

The ultimatum reached Tokyo on the morning of 27 July. It received a mixed reaction. The seventy-eight year old Prime Minister Suzuki was desperate for peace, but a peace that would protect the Emperor. Admiral Toyoda insisted it be rejected and the Cabinet agreed with him. On 28 July Suzuki replied to the Allied demands with the word *mokusatsu*, rejection.

The Americans concluded the Gumbutsu were still firmly in control and were determined to continue the war to a bitter conclusion; they therefore saw no alternative but to go ahead with the bombing. Orders were given for the first atomic attack.

There were four possible targets. Hiroshima, Niigata and Nagaski, which were all military complexes but also heavily populated, and Kyoto, the City of Temples. The latter city was eventually taken off the condemned list because of its long and important cultural history. Kokura was then substituted as a target. In fact, Kokura was to be the primary target until Intelligence reported that a prisoner-of-war camp had been constructed on the outskirts of the city. Hiroshima then became the primary target. In the end Niigata was removed from the target list as being too small and too far away. The target cities were deliberately spared from bombardment by American bombers which by 1945 could reconnoitre any target on the mainland they pleased without any resistance. This deceptive period of grace was given to the three cities so that their ruin would be all the more horrific and spectacular when destroyed by the new bomb.

The man given the responsibility of selecting the actual target, the date and timing of the attack and all other operational details was General Carl Spaatz, Commander of the Strategic Air Forces in the Pacific. He was to act in liaison with his Chief of Staff, General Curtis Le May. The attack itself would be led by Colonel Paul Tibbetts, a highly rated pilot with considerable operational experience. He was chosen because of his outstanding decision-making ability. His primary task was to work out a battle plan that would give him the optimum chance of getting safely through the Japanese defences and then ensuring an accurate drop on the target from a height of 30 000 feet.

There were considerable problems to overcome. The B-29 was an excellent bomber: sleek and stream-lined, its range, speed and ability to cruise at altitudes up to 40 000 feet, made it the ideal carrier for the Thin Man, but it was vulnerable to the Japanese Zero and also to ground attack. The Mitsubishi *A6M Zero* was a superlative fighter aircraft – fast, agile, with a high rate of climb, good range and heavy armament – all prime factors in the skies. It was this fighter that took such a heavy toll of the early, almost obsolete, British and American aircraft. A fighter escort could not guarantee the B-29 protection. Moreover, such an escort would draw attention to the attacking aircraft. At the time no-one was sure the bomb would work from the air and, if it did, what effect the explosion would have on the aircraft delivering the bomb. The fewer planes in the vicinity the better.

In view of the long flying distances involved, it was necessary to keep bombers as light as possible. Tibbetts figured that if he stripped the B-29 of most of its armour plating and all its guns, except one in the tail, at his height of 30 000 feet he would be as fast as the Zeroes and out of range of ground anti-aircraft fire. Normally the Superfortress carried a dozen 0.50 calibre machine guns and a 0.20 millimetre cannon. At a crew briefing this news that they would be going over Japan in an unprotected plane startled his battle-experienced crews. These men had been specially chosen on the basis of their battle record either in Europe or the Pacific. They had done an intensive course at Wendover Airfield in Utah, practising to hit a target from 30 000 feet with less than a 200 yard error. They had no inkling of what their eventual mission was to be. They could not understand the strange manoeuvres they had to practise. After dropping their bombs they had to make a sharp 160° turn, nosing the Superfortress sharply downward so as to gain maximum speed. What they did not know was that after dropping an atom bomb a plane must be at least eight miles away to escape the effects of the huge accompanying shock wave. Since coming to Tinian they had worked in the isolation of their compound and dispersal area. From here they would carry out sorties over Japan with single, large-calibre bombs. This was not only to test their accuracy in bombing from 30 000 feet, but also to accustom the enemy to seeing single aircraft, or sometimes formations of three, flying at great heights and dropping single bombs.

A total of seven B-29 Superforts were scheduled for the first delivery of the bomb. Three of these, leaving in advance, would take up weather stations over Hiroshima, Kokura and Nagasaki, reporting back to Tinian and Guam. This would give Colonel Tibbetts time enough during his approach run to select the city most suitable for a visual drop.

At all costs the bomb had to be dropped in good visibility with a clear sight of the target, so that the precise effect of the bomb could be seen. Tibbetts would then decide which target to bomb after receiving the weather reports. A fourth Superfortress was to be flown up to Iwojima, to stand by in case the bomb had to be jettisoned in the sea and the attack plane land there. Escorting Colonel Tibbetts' B-29 would be another two of the big bombers, one carrying scientists and monitoring instruments to measure the blast, the other observers and cameras. Cheshire and Robert Penney were to be two of the observers. Fighter aircraft would be operating at lower levels off the Japanese coast. Along the route a series of rescue vessels were standing by.

By the evening of 2 August the Thin Man had been assembled and was ready to be loaded into Tibbetts' plane. The bomb was torpedo-shaped, ten feet long, and just over two feet in diameter. Armed with its 135-pound uranium core and plug, it weighed almost four and a half tons. On its khaki-coloured body, armourers on Tinian had scrawled the usual graffiti in crayon: *Sod Tojo, For the Emperor,* and *Nip the Nips.* There was also a pin-up of a high-kicking Rita Hayworth.

One of the ordnance men had scribbled on the fins of the bomb a memorial to the dead sailors of the cruiser *Indianapolis,* torpedoed by a Japanese submarine. Tinian Island rumour had it that 900 of her 1200-man crew had died in the shark-infested waters of the Philippine Sea before the Navy knew she had been hit: the bomb might help to avenge them.

Inside the Thin Man's case was a half-ton six-inch gun barrel, six feet long. At one end was a charge of TNT and a uranium plug: at the other end the uranium core. Firing the plug into the core would create an instantaneous critical mass and an explosion estimated to be equivalent to 15 000 tons of TNT. The system – unlike that of the plutonium bomb tested three weeks before at Alamogorde – had never been tried.

Because of the many electronic and other complicated circuits needed to keep the bomb in a state of readiness a 'black box' was fitted to the aircraft to monitor how the circuits were functioning.

Finally zero hour – the time of the explosion of the bomb – was fixed for 08.15 hours 6 August. On the morning of 4 August, the seven participating crews were mustered to an initial briefing. For more than a year the crews of the B-29s had trained day and night for this one mission. Tibbetts told them the full destructive power of the bomb. They were shown movies of the test of the first atomic bomb test. This was their first inkling of what they were about to do. Suddenly their training techniques made sense. The solo raids, the dropping of only a single bomb. And that awful fireball, that soaring mushroom cloud; now they understood why again and again they had been forced to practise those swift, abrupt turns after the drop.

The briefing went on – radio frequencies etc., and all the other information vital for success. Tibbetts announced the three targets in order of priority. They were Hiroshima, Kokura and Nagasaki. Each city was warned of the impending attack. Admiral Leahy described this as the best kept secret of the war. Even General MacArthur, Supreme Commander of all Allied Forces in the Pacific, was not aware of what was about to happen. He and his staff officers were busy scrutinizing maps for the invasion of Japan.

The weather forecasts for 2 August and for the next three days were bad. But on 5 August the meteorologists predicted that the skies would be clear at dawn next day over the target cities.

Cheshire was disappointed when he was later told that he and Penney would not be on that first bombing mission. Perhaps it was decided to make it an all-American operation. However, he was assured that he and Penney would certainly be included as observers if the Fat Man was flown over Nagasaki, which would be bombed if the Japanese didn't surrender after the first attack, just to show that the Americans had a whole arsenal of atomic bombs in reserve. (In fact, they had not one more after the Fat Man.) A second bomb would surely induce surrender.

On the afternoon of 5 August, the operating crews were ordered to rest and sleep. But the weather was very hot and the steamy tents cut out neither the heat nor the light. They were issued with sleeping pills. But these didn't work until later. In fact, at the final night briefing at 23.00 hours, the crews had to be given Benzedrine to wake them up! The men strolled into the Mess for the customary midnight breakfast of fresh eggs, oatmeal, sausage and coffee, wished each other well and made for their individual aircraft, waiting, like sinister phantoms, to take them on their errand of death. It was time to go. The one (No. 82) carrying the Thin Man was the *Enola Gay*, named after the mother of the pilot, Colonel Paul Tibbetts, the only person who had supported his youthful ambition to become a flyer. He and his crew climbed into the heavily loaded plane. Sitting next to Tibbetts was his co-pilot, Captain Robert A. Lewis, who had earlier helped Tibbetts test B-29s. The navigator was Theodore Van Kirk, only twenty-three years old, but already one of the surest navigators in the Air Force. The bombardier was Major Thomas Ferebee, a soft-spoken North Carolinian with a huge moustache. The flight engineer was Technical Sergeant Wyatt E. Duzenbury, with Sergeant Robert Shumard as his assistant. Corporal Richard Nelson was the radio operator, Sergeant Joseph Stiborik the radar operator, and Staff Sergeant George Caron the tail gunner. They were all hand-picked men. In addition to this regular nine-man crew there were three others, necessitated by the nature of their special bomb-load: Navy Captain William Parsons, weaponeer; First Lieutenant Morris Jeppson, electronics officer; and Second Lieutenant Jacob Besar, radar counter-measures officer. The latter two stepped into the bucket seats in front of the 'black box'. Between them, these two would not, for the next seven hours, take their eyes off the dials monitoring the electronic circuits. There was always the possibility of the Japanese succeeding in detonating the bomb while it was still in the aircraft.

The bomb had not yet been armed. The previous night Captain Parsons, the ordnance expert for the technical firing of the bomb, had watched three main force B-29s crack-up on take-off. They had been carrying conventional 2000-pound mines for planting in the seas around the Japanese coast. The resulting explosions were frightening, leaving little of the planes or their crews. Parsons was not going to take any chances, especially as the *Enola Gay* was well beyond its safe take-off weight. He had just seen the film of the atom bomb test. He knew what would happen to Tinian and to everyone on it if the *Enola Gay* were to crack-up on take-off.

The bomb was set to explode at a height of 2000 feet, so as to cause maximum blast but minimum radiation. This required a complicated detonation mechanism, with no guarantee that it would work. Parsons decided he would prime the bomb after the *Enola Gay* was safely in the air and over the sea. Once the bomb had been primed the aircraft could not turn back.

For the remainder of that afternoon and until late into the night, Parsons practised the delicate operation of arming the Thin Man. The main core of fissionable uranium 235 was in its nose. In its tail was another small chunk of U_{235}. While the two pieces of uranium were separated they were quite harmless - they had not reached their critical mass. But when a fuse went off it would trigger a conventional charge of explosive that would fire the small piece of uranium into the other piece of uranium: the critical mass would be exceeded and an atomic explosion would result. Placing the conventional explosive charge into position so that it would activate the bomb at the proper time - and doing it by flashlight in the bay of the Superfortress - was the delicate task Parsons had set for himself.

Suddenly there was a mighty roar that shattered the silence of the whole island as, one by one, the engines of the huge Superfortresses started up. Cheshire and Penney covered their ears against the deafening crescendo. At 01.37 hours on 6 August the trio of weather planes took off on separate runways, one bound for Hiroshima, one for Kokura, one for Nagasaki.

At 02.45 hours the *Enola Gay*, with the Thin Man tucked into its belly, shook and rattled as the four powerful engines strained to free the great ship from the wheel brakes. The whirring propellors cut four circles of light against the black night, as it waited, like a sprinter at the starting blocks, at the head of the coral runway.

On a separate runway to his right stood the plane nicknamed the *Great Artiste*, ready poised, with its cargo of technical equipment and its team of scientists led by Luis Alvarez. Major Charles Sweeney acknowledged the 'thumbs up'. The capsule containing the monitoring instruments was to be dropped one mile behind the Thin Man. To the left, on another runway, stood Number 91, the *Straight Flush*, the camera and photographic plane, with Major Ellerby at the controls. In the distance the tall palms stood silent, heads bowed, all the world like silver wraiths in the Pacific darkness, sombre witnesses to the impending drama.

High above hung the bright sliver of the newest of new moons, marking the death of the old and heralding the birth of the new. The moon has always played an important role in Japanese literature and culture. Was this thin crescent announcing that the old order was about to die and a new, greater phase of meaning was about to begin, however cataclysmic the introduction?

Tibbetts looked at his watch. Ten seconds to go. Everyone was in his special place in the 99-feet long cigar-shaped B-29, waiting for the twelve-hour 3000-mile flight that lay ahead. He spoke into his microphone.

'Dimples Eight Two to Tinian Tower. Ready for take off.'

Back came the reply through his headphone. 'Tinian Tower to Dimples Eight Two. Cleared for take off.'

Tibbetts released the brakes and eased forward on the throttle for full power. The 65-ton weight of the *Enola Gay* moved sluggishly at first, then began to pick up speed to 180 miles per hour as the 10 000 feet of runway unrolled itself beneath the massive wheels. No lift off yet. The precious yards of runway streamed away. But Tibbetts knew what he was doing. He held the giant Superfortress on the ground until the last possible moment, with only a few yards of coral left, letting the 8800 horse-power in the engines build up steadily. He eased back on the wheel and the plane broke upwards and headed into the air over the sequinned Pacific waters, past the hills of Saipan on the right, for a destination a thousand miles away. All being well it would be over the target at 08.15 a.m., zero hour. One by one the other giant bombers thundered off. With excitement tinged with disappointment Cheshire and Penney watched the flaming exhausts get smaller and smaller as they disappeared to become indistinguishable from the shining constellations about them. By the time the two would have their next meal the course of the history of the planet would have been changed irrevocably.

Tibbetts took the plane up to 4000 feet and throttled the engines back to cruising speed. He set the compass heading north by north-west for Iwo Jima and turned the controls over to Captain Lewis, his co-pilot. At 03.00 hours Parsons began the difficult and dangerous task of arming the Thin Man, the single bomb that had cost more than $10 000 million dollars to make. He and Jeppson lowered themselves into the bomb bay. At least the air there was cool. While Jeppson held the flashlight, Parsons reached gingerly through the tail of the bomb and, while they both held their breath, directed the explosive detonating charge into place. Then it was Jeppson's turn. He extended his arm and carefully worked free a green plug out of the Thin Man's side. He replaced it with a red one that fitted flush with the casing. That completed the electric circuits. The Thin Man was primed for its rendezvous with Armageddon.

part two

Pika-Don

Chapter Four

A kind of respite

Hiroshima, early morning, 6 August 1945

Toshiko was a pretty young lass, just twenty years old. She was not as bright and bubbling as her usual self. But, then, no one is at three o'clock in the morning. She had been woken earlier by the thunderous roar of aeroplanes passing overhead. At midnight the city's radio had announced that some 200 American B-29s were approaching Japan's southern island of Kyushu. Citizens were advised to evacuate to their designated safe areas. But Hiroshima had been getting air-raid warnings almost every night for weeks. Many people just ignored the warnings. Night after night the B-29s streamed in over the coast near the city. They would rendezvous above Lake Biwa, north-east of Hiroshima and then fly off to their targets. One night in March of that year 334 B-29s had crossed the coast, rendezvoused and then made for Tokyo. They came in below 5000 feet. The Japanese fighters, the few that remained, stayed on the ground. They were being held in reserve as *kamikaze* fighters when the invasion of Japan took place.

Out of the velvet, undefended sky poured hundreds of thousands of six-pound M-69 incendiary bombs, containing the recently developed napalm, on Tokyo's wood-and-rice-paper houses. Not even the Imperial Palace was spared. In minutes the city was a crematorium, a strong wind fanning the deadly firestorms. Approximately 267 000 houses were flattened, 2300 city blocks incinerated. Fire-fighting forces were overwhelmed. Men, women and children struggling to escape the flames jammed the city's narrow alleys and humpbacked little foot-bridges, where their charred bodies remained piled for days. Beneath the bridges floated corpses boiled in canals which had bubbled from the heat. More than 90 000 men, women and children perished. Another 41 000 were wounded. Over a million slept homeless in the ruins. In May the B-29s struck again. The area set on fire was even greater. Japanese guards allowed sixty-two American POWs in the Tokyo Military Prison to burn, while 400 Japanese prisoners were saved. A few weeks later Kobe was reduced to rubble, with more than 35 000 people burned alive. Then Yokohama, Osaka, Nagoya, were gutted by the firebombs. No wonder that Foreign Minister Shigemitsu remarked that 'day by day

Japan turned into a furnace.' Nearer to home there had been mass raids on Kure, Iwakuni, Tokuyama and other nearby towns.

Normally Toshiko would get up at seven, in time to get to her work as a clerk in the personnel department of the East Asia Tin Works at Kannonmachi. But today she had more than a full share of domestic duties. Not only did she have to prepare breakfast for her father, brother, a sister and herself but also a whole day's meals for her mother and an eleven-month old baby brother, Akio, who were in hospital. Akio had gone down with a serious stomach ailment and her mother had taken him to the Tamura Paediatric Hospital where she would be staying and looking after him. It was the custom in Japan that when a person fell ill and went to hospital, one or more members of the family would go and live in the hospital, as a *tsukisoi*, so as to do the cooking, bathing, reading and other chores for the patient, providing round-the-clock family support and sympathy. The Japanese had a saying: *i wa jinjutsu* – 'medicine is the art of compassion'.

Toshiko looked across at the little, red, fat man – her *dharma* doll – sitting on the kitchen ledge. She smiled at the pleasure her gift was going to bring to Akio that morning. A *dharma* doll was a small figure of a man, lacquered red, on a rounded base: if he were pushed over he would immediately return to his erect position. It was said of these dolls *Nana-korobi-ya-oki*: if you are knocked down seven times, you will get up at eight.

Pushing back her black hair she gave the *ozoni* soup another stir and then began to pat together the *mochi*, rice cakes, on her *hibachi* charcoal stove. Today she would give her family a special treat; she packed *sashimi* (tuna) into their *o-bento* (lunch box).

She thought about her fiancé. Where was he now? When would he return from war service in China? Three years ago her parents had entered into marriage negotiations with his parents, as was the custom. They had all met the proposed young man once, at a meeting arranged by a *nakodo*, a marriage go-between.

The dawn was breaking now. She opened the window and placed some crumbs on the sill for the birds. As a good Buddhist she believed that birds and butterflies were the re-incarnation of good people, whereas horses or oxen were the re-incarnation of bad people.

The smell of night soil, used as fertilizer, wafted in through the window. She laid out the rice bowls and the chopsticks for her family. She partook of the traditional Japanese breakfast of bean-paste soup, rice with flakes of sea-weed, and green tea with a sweet bean pastry. Her tiny feet pattered over the *tatami* straw mat. She looked into the mirror. She brushed off a loose lock of hair that lined her starched white blouse. She crammed her tiny feet into the *zori* straps of her sandals, picked up her quilted air-raid hood and her *furoshiki*, a square of coloured cloth used by the Japanese to carry things, and bowed to the family picture on the altar on the family shrine. She bowed even lower as she prayed to Ama-Terasu, the Sun Goddess. Below the Zen* Buddhist layers of their national culture there was firmly embedded in the Japanese Shinto form of ancestor worship the story of their descent from Ama-Terasu, the goddess of the sun. The sacred personage of the Emperor was a direct descendant of Ama-Terasu.

Toshiko glided out of her home in Koi, through the little family rock garden, into the thoroughfare, already abustle with pedestrians and cyclists and trams and buses and charcoal-burning army lorries spewing the foulest black smoke into the atmosphere. She bowed low as she passed a large statue of the Buddha, a large jewel in the forehead. Unlike the rational truths of science, for Buddhists the higher truths are seen by the eyes of the heart. That is why many images of Buddha have a jewel in the head, which is 'the eye of the heart', which sees beyond mere appearances. She prayed the *Nenbutsu*, the common prayer of Japanese Buddhism: *Namu Amida Butsu*: 'we depend on you utterly, Amida Buddha'.

୨ଓ

The sound of an aircraft in the distance woke Father Arrupe. He opened one eye. The Jesuit priest was no longer in prison. After some weeks in solitary confinement he had been released: there was no evidence to prove he was a Western spy. The dawn was just breaking through his open *shoji* screen, made of light lattice and opaque white paper. The drone was bang on time. It was 4.30 a.m. Every day at this time, regular as clockwork, an American B-29 bomber appeared in the sky, presumably on a reconnaissance mission. One had no need of an alarm clock. This 'clock' gave him enough time to prepare for the 5.30 Mass. Father Arrupe often marvelled at the precision timing of this reconnaissance plane. He wondered how good its precision bombing would be if it ever changed to that. So far it had never come to that. Indeed, it was strange that whilst most of the cities round about Hiroshima had been flattened by hundreds of B-29 bombers, Hiroshima itself had not been touched. It was because of these bombings elsewhere that many of the Jesuit priests and novices in Tokyo had recently been evacuated to the comparative safety of Hiroshima. The Jesuit Novitiate in Hiroshima was now full to bursting.

---

* Zen is a strict form of Buddhism in which meditation plays the key role.

Militarily, however, Hiroshima was of great strategic importance. It was the main military centre of South Japan. It was the second General Headquarters for the Japanese forces. It would become the Imperial Headquarters if the islands were invaded and Tokyo capitulated. Huge stocks of military supplies were hidden in the surrounding countryside. Hiroshima was one of the principal ports for shipping armed forces to Japan's now slowly but steadily decreasing empire. Each week thousands of soldiers embarked from the port of Ujina. Heavy industrial plants ringed the city. Some thought Hiroshima had not been attacked because of the pleas of those emigrants from the city now living in the United States and Hawaii for their city to be spared. Others, more percipiently, believed the city had been spared because the Americans were preparing something special for it.

After Mass Father Arrupe went into the garden. It was a bright, clear, summer morning, just a few cumulus flecking the sky. The air was fresh and clean. Dew still clung to the red flowers of the sycamores and the camellias that grew in abundance in the garden tended so lovingly by the novices. He made a special point of inhaling deep the sweet fragrance of the many flowers, the azalea, iris, rhododendron, blue anemone. He gazed with increasing awe at the wonderful colours of the delicate flowers and leaves. His weeks in solitary confinement in Yamaguchi prison had taught him to appreciate nature to the full. Even such a common sight as the terraced rice-fields beyond now held a special magic for him.

At 6.00 a.m. the air-raid siren went off – a series of intermittent blasts – indicating only a slight degree of danger. About 7.00 a.m. the familiar one minute long 'Ooo' of the air-raid sirens again broke the quiet of the bright, peaceful, morning. A few planes appeared over the city. No one paid any attention to the warning sirens. Observation planes over the city were a daily, routine, occurrence. Everybody continued about their business as usual. Most people treated the planes with total indifference, even making fun of them as the 'American air mail'. Indeed, two days earlier American B-29s had dropped thousands of leaflets on the city, warning the people that if Japan did not surrender, the city would be destroyed by a bomb too horrendous to contemplate. They should evacuate the city. The people ignored this as just propaganda.

At 7.55 a lone B-29 appeared over the city. The air-raid warning was totally ignored, as usual. At 8.00 a.m. the All Clear sounded. The enemy plane had left the city. By now the midsummer sun was climbing into the eastern sky and beating down pitilessly. A little boy and a little girl, presumably his sister, called out a greeting to Arrupe as they skipped their way, hands clasped together, along the path on their way to school. Children often used the path as a short-cut to the school. Air-raid warnings or no, the children would not be missing school. Japan paid great attention to the education of its children. There was no illiteracy in Japan; all children knew how to read and write; all children went to primary and then secondary school.

Both children were carrying their large, home-made, padded, cotton air-raid helmets, called *bokuzuki*, as a precaution in the event of air-raids. *Bokuzuki* were compulsory equipment to be carried at all times by people outside. The boy wore pants and a shirt; his sister a cotton dress. First-aid kits hung from their shoulders; their lunch boxes they carried in their hands. They both wore no shoes or socks. In the summer this was no great hardship. But even in winter children would go to school barefooted and without underwear, shivering from the cold, as their contribution towards conserving materials that might be needed for the nation's war effort. They would be hungry, too. The meals consisted just of rice and fish, with beans, squash, sweet potatoes and even weeds when the food was insufficient.

Suddenly the little boy stopped and shaded his eyes as he peered into the sky above. His sister followed him.

'Look, *Shinspu-sama* (Father), *B-san*,' the boy, shouted, pointing heavenward with his finger. '*B-san*' or 'Mr B' was how the Japanese referred to the B-29s, with a mixture of familiarity and respect.In those days the B-29s flying overhead were so common children referred to them as though they were little pets. They were probably too young to imagine the 'pets' opening their bomb bays. Glinting like foil in the sunlight, the two B-29s made a lovely sight, as they chalked straight white double contrails across the blue.

The wing of one of the B-29s flashed in the sunlight as it banked to its left. The plane rolled from its turn and began to inch east again, towards the Inland Sea and the ocean beyond. He presumed it was a reconnaissance plane, photographing the shore-line for the coming invasion landings, or, maybe, it was checking the weather for the other *B-sans* waiting to begin their day's assaults on the Japanese mainland.

The two children waved and continued on their way, skipping as they went. The spare middle-aged Jesuit, with his high, domed forehead and with a slight beak to his nose, resembling in appearance the founder of his Order, Saint Ignatius Loyola, waved back and made for his study.

In the centre of the city, Nobori-cho, the Jesuits had another House and Church. Father Wilhelm Kleinsorge, one of the priests at the Mission, felt frail. The Japanese wartime diet of rice, beans, parched peas and fish had not sustained him. For two days now he had suffered from a painful and urgent diarrhoea. He blamed this on the beans and black ration bread he was obliged to eat. Also, the strain of being a *gaijin*, a foreigner, in an increasingly xenophobic country, was beginning to take its toll. As a German he was nominally an ally. But after the defeat of the Fatherland the Japanese cared little about their former ally. He was thirty-eight and had the look of a boy growing too fast – thin in the face, with a prominent Adam's apple, a hollow chest, dangling hands and big feet.

That morning he was up at six as usual. Half-an-hour later he began Mass in the mission chapel. The chapel was a small Japanese-style wooden building. There were no pews for the worshippers; they would kneel on the usual *tatami*-matted floor, facing an altar decked with silks and embroideries, brass and silver candlesticks.

This Monday morning there were not many in the congregation. There were his fellow priests – Father Superior La Salle, Father Schiffer, Father Cieslik and a fourth-year theology student, Mr Takemoto. Also present were Mr Fukai, the secretary of the diocese and Mrs Mureta, the mission's devoutly Christian housekeeper.

At the end of Mass, while Father Kleinsorge was reading the Prayers of Thanksgiving, there was the long 'Ooo' moan of the sirens, warning of approaching aircraft. The priests finished their prayers and then moved across the compound to the Mission House, a big, three-storey building. Father Kleinsorge entered a room on the ground floor of the House and changed into military uniform. He always did this during air-raid alerts in case he was called out for special duties. He went outside and, shading his eyes from the blinding sun, scanned the dazzlingly blue sky. The summer sun was high above the mountains which ran round three sides of the city. You could feel the humidity like a fever. Only a single plane flew across the sky. He assumed this was the usual weather plane carrying out its daily routine. He went inside again and joined his colleagues in breakfast of substitute coffee and the unpalatable bread. At eight o'clock the all-clear sounded. They all dispersed.

Father Superior La Salle stood at the window of his room, going over the day's programme. Father Schiffer sat down to his writing. Father Cieslik sat in his room with a pillow over his stomach: he, too, was afflicted with severe diarrhoea. Father Kleinsorge slowly climbed the wooden stairs to his room on the third floor. He took off his uniform, standing only in his underwear. He lay down on his cot and began reading *Stimmen der Zeit*, a Jesuit magazine – albeit an old copy since the magazine had been suppressed by the Nazis in 1943.

♌︎℞

By now the city's sprawling community of 245 000 people was awake. The *tenshu* tower of Hiroshima Castle, appropriately flying the flag of the rising sun, soared, five storeys high, in clean, white splendour, into the blue sky, dwarfing the wood and tiled buildings at its feet. This large, feudal redoubt had been built in 1589 by Lord Mowri Terumoto, in the fashion of a massive, broad-based pagoda. Its uppermost storey was a perfectly square house, crowned with a green tiled roof. The Castle housed 4000 troops of the Chugoku Regional Military Headquarters. Large carp swam hungrily in the sapphire moat that surrounded the Castle.

In a segregated section of the barracks in the Castle a group of US prisoners-of-war – those who were able to stand – lined up, barefoot, on the gravel, their smelly khaki shirts tucked into baggy, tattered khaki shorts, their emaciated arms holding out rice bowls. Gaunt, hungry eyes stared out of haggard faces at the guard who went down the ragged line slopping a disgusting mixture of evil smelling fish on top of stale, equally evil-smelling, rice. One prisoner held out two bowls – one for a colleague who had been beaten up that night by one of the guards for calling him a 'Nip'. The man doing the slopping of food hit the second bowl to the ground and passed on. The men, like ghosts, shuffled off and sat in the courtyard picking the morsels from their rice bowls with their hands.

One poor fellow couldn't open his mouth. He had suffered an *aiki* kick to the jaw for not bowing with sufficient alacrity in the direction of the rising sun. They were never given any news of the war, except that the American pigs were being hammered by the heroic Japanese and that the unjust war started by American capitalists would soon be over. The prisoners had every reason to believe what they were told. They never heard any planes bombing the city. Perhaps that was just as well, for they would be sitting ducks for their own pilots. They did not know what had happened to the American POWs in prison in Tokyo.

On the East Drill Parade Ground, a few blocks from the Castle, troops were mustering for the morning roll call. A major, a single silver star shining on each red tab at his tunic collar, a curved *tachi* sword with a diamond-laced hilt hanging from a leather belt polished to a glitter, directed operations. The flash of *katanas*, the grunt of combat, came from small groups practising the martial arts. An officer, his cap pulled low over his head to keep out the sun's glare, a *samurai* sword hanging down his left trouser and reaching well below the top of his leather jack-boot, demonstrated how a spear could be used to inflict maximum damage.

A corporal had obviously found fault with the set of a man's cap. He bawled out abuse, slapping the man as he did so. The cap curved in a parabolic arc into the gravel. The private bowed low to the corporal, broke ranks, picked up the offending headgear, dusted it, replaced it, bowed low again and rejoined the ranks.

'Turn to the north east,' the corporal shouted.

The ranks turned half-right face, to face Tokyo, 350 miles away.

'Revere the Imperial Palace.'

The men bowed low, sliding stiff palms down their trousers, till their backs were horizontal.

'Return to Attention.'

'Recite the Five Imperial Doctrines!'

The sun beat down. It was stiflingly hot. The officers wore their shirt collars open outside their jackets. Wounded veterans, some still on crutches, drilled a motley crowd of middle-aged men, wielding wooden rifles. A group of women, in their baggy *monpe* pantaloons, loose blouses, and coloured bandannas round their heads, practised their expertise with bamboo spears. A General Mobilisation Ordinance required all females between thirteen and sixty to undertake regular bamboo spear practice. They were to fight the invading Americans like the wives, children and grandmothers of the *samurai* of old who fought to the death when a threat arose. There was no doubt that when the invasion of the mainland came every man, woman and child would fight to the bitter end. The Ministry of Propaganda had painted the Americans in dripping blood: they would rape, pillage, murder and exterminate the peace-loving Japanese. Posters showed American Marines bayoneting helpless women and children.

In the schools, too, the children, dressed in the tan uniforms of the Student Labour Force, were practising their drills and martial arts. All junior and senior high school students were required to alternate their academic activities with national service. This consisted primarily of assisting the demolition crews on the House Clearance Project. Most of the houses consisted of a wooden frame and wooden walls supporting a heavy tile roof. In order to reduce the risk from incendiary bombs, houses in crowded districts were being demolished so as to make wide lanes between houses as fire-breaks. Only yesterday school children had helped a patriotic baker pull down his own little shop which stood in the path of a projected municipal fire lane. At Zakoba-cho Junior College girl students were singing cheerfully as they carried away roof tiles, passing them along from one to the other. At Honkawa School the boys were doing their drill with wooden rifles. In the afternoon they would be engaged on agricultural work or on the House Clearance Project.

Downtown, the streets teamed with life as usual in the hot morning sun. Some Junior Air Cadets swaggered past, their seven brass buttons gleaming, acknowledging the bows of the passers by. There were hardly any cars or taxis any more, but the streets were already busy with bicycle traffic. Streetcars clanged past, bursting with passengers. Hangers-on even clung to the cow-catchers at the rear. A group of women heading for work in the fields shuffled past lustily singing 'Blossoms and Buds of the Young Cherry Tree.'

For those indoors, the radio announced that 'enemy planes are now advancing north from the Bungo Narrows.' But almost immediately the all-clear sounded. At 8.06 a volunteer plane watcher at the Matsunaga look-out station in the hills to the east of Hiroshima sighted two B-29s flying very high and heading north-east towards the city. He picked up his telephone and began reporting them when he spotted another, following some miles behind. He included this one also in his report to the Prefecture Air Alert Station. The Air Alert Station passed on the message to Chugoku Regional Military Headquarters. The Second Army Headquarters always received advance notice so as to give officers time enough to put any classified documents into their safes.

A soldier manning earphones at the Nakano searchlight battery's sound-detection equipment, near Hiroshima, picked up the drone of aircraft engines at 8.14 a.m. Training his huge mechanical ear, he reported that unidentified aircraft were approaching from Saijo, fifteen miles east of Hiroshima, and heading for the centre of the city.

At 8.15 two planes were sighted by anti-aircraft spotters of a battery on Mukay-Shima Island in Hiroshima Harbour. They were B-29s, one following the other, but separating rapidly. Anti-aircraft shells were piled up by the sand-bagged guns. But the planes were flying six miles high. Anti-aircraft fire would have been futile. The sergeant commanding the battery decided to hold fire and the gunners could only watch.

The two aircraft acted oddly. When the first was almost a half mile ahead of the other, it banked violently toward the right. At the same time, the second aircraft banked left: below it two tiny parachutes blossomed white against the blue. The men in the Mukay-Shima battery let out a cheer: obviously, the second plane was in some kind of trouble and the crew was bailing out.

51

A group of factory workers from the Mitsubishi Works were pedalling along merrily on their bicycles.

'B-san,' one of them shouted, pointing upwards with his left hand.

Some others looked up as well. Then suddenly they all stopped pedalling and dismounted.

'Look! Something's dropped from that plane,'one of the men shouted. They also cheered and clapped, a few even threw their cloth caps in the air, as they saw the two parachutes descend from one of the planes. The crew of one of the B-29s had baled out! The men on the ground rejoiced. And what would they do to the crew when they touched land! The men kept gazing up at the parachutes.

While the men on the ground were gazing up into the sky, Major Thomas Ferebee, a poker-playing Southerner, was looking down on them from a height of 30 000 feet. He was the bombardier aboard the *Enola Gay*.

Chapter Five

Pika-Don

6 August 1945

The *Enola Gay*, carrying the Thin Man, had set off from the tiny island of Tinian at 02.45 that morning, 6 August 1945. Accompanied by two escorting B-29s, Special Bombing Mission 13 had droned north along the Hirohito Highway to an as-yet-undecided final target city on the island of Honshu. The red lights in the cockpit indicating that the bomb was live had been glowing for over two hours when the island of Iwo Jima slipped by in the black ocean below as the B-29 flew on auto-pilot. The darkness hid the scars of the recent bloody, hand-to-hand fighting between the Japanese defenders and the US Marines. The *Enola Gay* was beginning the final leg of her journey, as Colonel Tibbetts headed the Superfortress toward Shikoku, an island off the southeast tip of Japan. He began the long climb up to near bombing altitude, six miles high. Jeppson and Parsons, their eyes still glued on the 'black box' in front of them, were reassured by the green lights; everything was in order. Presently pink streaks in the sky heralded another dawn.

At 07.09 the *Straight Flush*, the accompanying weather plane, was in sight of Hiroshima. The solid undercover of cloud suddenly broke, as if on command, and the city below came into view through a huge opening in the sky, as if waiting for the *Enola Gay*'s fateful cargo. Radio Operator Baldasaro sent his coded weather report:

'Cloud cover less than three tenths at all altitudes. Advice: Bomb primary.'

At 07.42 Tibbetts announced over the inter-com: 'It's Hiroshima.'

At 07.50 the *Enola Gay* was over Shikoku Island. The crew began climbing into their flak suits. Radar was turned off and Tibbetts took over manual control of the Superfortress. By 08.06 he was over Fukuyama Bay. Below a convoy of ships steamed north. He began a gradual climb from 26 000 feet to bombing altitude and then levelled off at 31 000 feet.

At 08.09 Tibbetts began his bombing run. Depending on the speed of the aircraft, its height, the angle of fall of the bomb, the run-up must be several miles from the aiming point. In this case it was seventeen miles ahead. Allowing for the Enola Gay's altitude of 30 000 feet the bomb would be released three-and-a-half miles before the target point was reached. Below him the seventh largest city in Japan basked in the sun through a ten-mile hole in the clouds, as though the god of war was providing a beacon for the Thin Man.

'Put on your goggles,' he announced. 'Here we go!'

All but three of the crew – Ferebee, Jeppson and Parsons – pulled down their heavy polaroid sunglasses. Major Ferebee climbed into the Plexiglas nose of the Superfortress to fix the crosswires of the Norden bombsight on to his target – the city's T-shaped Aioi Bridge. He carefully adjusted the focus. Under the crosshairs the city spread before him like a relief map.

Hiroshima was a fan-shaped city, lying mostly on six islands formed by seven deltaic rivers that branch out from the River Ohta. The name Hiroshima derived from 'broad island' (*hiro* meaning broad; *shima* meaning island). The main commercial and residential districts, covering about four square miles in the centre of the city, contained three-quarters of its population, which had been reduced by several evacuation programmes from a wartime peak of 380 000 to about 245 000. Factories and other residential districts or suburbs lay compactly around the edges of the city. Hiroshima was proud of its folk-crafts. Wax-paper and umbrella factories abounded. So did the *sake* breweries. To the south of the city, were the docks, the airport and the island-studded Inland Sea. The bay teemed with the famous Hiroshima delicacy – oysters.

Off the coast the drowned hulk of the aircraft carrier *Amagi* could be seen with her flight deck awash and listing at forty-five degrees in the oily harbour swell. She had been there for two weeks. One could make out the Hall of Triumph at the port of Ujina, from which soldiers had sailed to conquer an empire overseas. They would be *banzai*-ed off with *sake* and assurances of quick victory. Neighbourhood Associations would be there to see that each 'rookie' left with a good showing of well-wishers waving Rising Sun flags and singing patriotic songs. But not now. The harbour was sewn with American mines dropped by B-29s; it had been empty of troop transports for a year now. Creaking side by side in the tide at the city's piers were hundreds of navy launches, packed with explosives. These were the suicide torpedo boats, waiting for the time when *kamikaze* sailors would drive them into any American landing craft. A rim of pine-green mountains circled the other three sides of the delta.

In the precise centre of Hiroshima, the Ohta River split into two branches: the Honkawa, flowing south west past the Honkawa Middle School, and the Motoyasu, flowing south east. Both continued for some thirty blocks before they passed the Hiroshima shipyard and army docks at Ujina and spilled into the Inland Sea. Crossing the

Ohta River where it split was a concrete four-lane bridge carrying a streetcar line. The bridge was the Aioi, and in its middle, at right angles to the main structure, another span jutted south to the teeming Tenjimachi District in the fork of the two river branches. Thus Aioi Bridge was T-shaped. Its unusual plan, in the middle of downtown Hiroshima and less than 800 yards from Second Army Headquarters and the Hiroshima military barracks, made it a perfect aiming point – almost a crosshair itself – for the Thin Man.

The laboratory plane, with its recording instruments, fell off at a thousand yards and the camera plane began a huge circle until it was time for it to take pictures – if any. Ferebee could see his target perfectly. When he had been shown the T-bridge on a reconnaissance photograph in Guam he recalled it was the most perfect aiming point he had seen in the war. And he had seen a lot of war. He was a veteran of the Berlin air-raids.

At 08.13 Tibbetts transferred control of the plane to Ferebee. Ferebee twiddled the fine focus with his fingers.

'I have it,' he shouted to Tibbetts over the intercom.

He locked the crosshairs of the bombsight on the T-bridge and triggered the automatic synchronization for the final minute of the run. Forty-five seconds later he started the radio tone signal that indicated only fifteen seconds remained to the drop. The final fifteen seconds were automatic.

At 08.15 plus 17 seconds the bomb doors swung open and the Thin Man began its descent, wobbling a little at first until it picked up speed. It arched down silently on the unsuspecting city below lying with its palm outstretched, like a schoolboy's awaiting the cane, or like Christ's waiting for the Roman centurion's nail to pierce his wrist, the fingers etched by the seven silvery branches of the Ohta River. At the same instant Tibbetts threw the *Enola Gay* into a violent 160-degree turn to the right and nosed down to gain speed. He had just forty-three seconds in which to get away far enough before the bomb would explode 1800 feet above the target. A trio of parachutes fell from the laboratory plane carrying the monitoring instruments which would transmit readings back to the plane. The parachutes fluttered open and floated down to earth gracefully, the measuring instruments dangling from them in canisters. (It was these parachutes which misled the Japanese onlookers on the ground to think that the crewmen were baling out.) Tibbetts straightened out so as to reduce the speed of the *Enola Gay*, hoping to reduce the impact of the anticipated shock wave.

The supersonic scream of the Thin Man never reached the ears of the people on the ground. For fifteen seconds the bomb fell. Then the barometric pressure gauges alerted the radio proximity fuses which had been timed to set the bomb off at 1850 feet above ground. Hopefully, at that point, all circuits would be in harmony, signals meshing in a fraction of a fraction of a single second.

At 1800 feet the barometric pressure triggered the detonating mechanism. Then, in fractions of a millisecond, it happened: *Pika-Don – Pika*, the lightning flash of the nuclear chain reaction and *Don*, the thunderous shock-wave. The early morning sunshine paled into insignificance as the bomb exploded in a blinding flash, which became an engulfing ball of flame and destruction.

A shock wave hit the Superfortress with a terrifying force, as if in retaliation. The B-29 bucked and trembled. To the men inside it felt as if the sleek fuselage was being battered mercilessly by forge hammers. And then came a second, angry, retaliatory shock-wave. This time the crew were better prepared for it.

The bomb exploded directly over the Shima Hospital in downtown Hiroshima and 800 feet away from Aioi Bridge. 320 000 men, women, and children were within forty blocks of Shima Hospital at 8.15 a.m., including 3200 American citizens of Japanese ancestry – mostly students – who were trapped in Hiroshima by the war. There was a tremendous flash of light, like lightning that shot across the sky from the east to west, from the city towards the hills, capable of destroying the retina of anyone looking at it. Those looking up at the parachutes, like the anti-aircraft gunners and the Mitsubishi workers, were blinded. The dazzling light bleached everything it touched. Any object, plant, animal or human, that happened to be in front of a flat surface cast a 'shadow', an unbleached area on a whitened background. On the concrete balustrade of Aioi Bridge – Major Ferebee's aiming point, which survived – the shadows of two people running and of a cyclist were etched, like graffiti. The heat from the explosion was tremendous, thousands of degrees hotter than the surface of the sun, a blast that seared through the city, melting roof tiles, charring telephone poles, incinerating everything within radius. A man and his horse-drawn cart were incinerated as they crossed the Sakai Bridge. Man, horse and cart left a shadow on the seared bridgework which showed the man's arm raised in the act of striking his horse. A painter on a ladder was monumentalized in a bas relief on the stone facade of a bank building on which he was working, in the very act of dipping his brush into a can of paint.

Some 700 yards away the heat had reduced a crowded streetcar to a tangle of buckled steel and welded its wheels to the tracks. The passengers were never seen again: they just vanished. At the moment when the bomb burst a Korean prince was riding out of Hiroshima

Castle, with cavalry escort, to inspect the parade. Prince, escort, horses and the parading soldiers were instantly vaporized. So was the entire Pioneer Regiment which had its barracks nearby. The five-storey Castle was reduced to its foundations. The great stones on which it was built had been welded together centuries ago with molten lead. The lead remelted and ran out into the street in red hot rivulets. Unprotected citizens near ground zero were vaporized, others liquefied, their fatty tissue melted as lard is rendered into soap. The tremendous heat not only scorched the skin but also tattooed into the skin the design of the clothing worn, as photographic images are transferred from negatives to print.

The bomb exploded with a force of 17 000 tons of TNT. The half-second shock-wave was the equivalent of a thousand-pound air hammer striking the human body at the speed of sound: it disembowelled those near, ruptured the ear drums of others, turned bodies into projectiles, filled the air with flying glass and stripped virtually all unsheltered victims of their clothing.

The bomb destroyed 60 000 of Hiroshima's 90 000 buildings, but, ironically, less than 26 percent of its industrial and military capacity, since industrial plants and army depots were on the periphery of the city. As far as four miles away houses collapsed and caught fire. Even nine miles away windows were broken. What did the greatest damage was the blast. The bomb was like a giant fly swatter two miles broad, slapped down on a city of flimsy, termite-eaten and dry-rotted wooden houses and rickety brick buildings, top-heavy with thick tile roofs, that sprawled, eave to eave, across the delta. Except for some large, modern, buildings of reinforced concrete, most of Hiroshima was built in the traditional Japanese style – most of the houses were built of hard woods, one storey high, though some were two storeys high; the fragile walls were made of thick paper and the floors of *tatami* or straw. The blast flattened them in one blow, burying perhaps 200 000 people in debris.

Fires flared simultaneously in thousands of places, caused by electrical short circuits, overturned stoves, kerosene lamps and broken gas mains. The bomb had struck at a time when the first meal of the day was being prepared in the kitchens. The flames, on making contact with the electric current wires, had turned the city into a gigantic sea of fire. In no time at all these combustible materials of wood, paper and straw went up in one fantastic bonfire. In incendiary attacks, people have some chance of escape. They run from their houses into the streets, to open places, to the rivers. In Hiroshima the majority had no such chance. Thousands of them were killed outright by falling walls and roofs; the rest were pinned down in a burning hell. Some 60000, it is estimated, were burned to death.

Out of a population of 245 000 it is thought that between 70 to 100 000 people died instantly: they were dead before they knew it, snuffed out in the blink of an eyelid. Few of them were ever identified. Hiroshima's elementary and middle schools, unlike her factories, were downtown, so some twenty thousand of those killed were children. Within four days the total dead reached 250000, as the mortally wounded died of burns, lacerations, and the early stages of radiation sickness. Over 30 000 citizens were severely injured but survived. Another 50000 escaped with only slight injuries. Five miles from Shima Hospital ten American B-29 crewmen who had baled out and been captured on 27 July in Kyushu died in their prison cells. Thirteen other American POWs in various military prisons throughout the city also died.

Colonel Tibbetts turned back the *Enola Gay* to see what had happened. In front of their very eyes the city of Hiroshima had disappeared. A moment before there had been nothing to distinguish Hiroshima from other cities of the world. A moment later it had gone, blown apart from the centre.

The original explosion turned into a vast fireball which slowly became dense smoke, 2000 feet above the ground, half a mile in diameter and rocketing upwards at 20 000 feet a minute into the cloudless sky. Smoke and flames were drawing up the entire city into a monstrous black cloud. The black ugly mushroom cloud lifted itself to 60 000 feet where it remained stationary, a good two miles in diameter, sulphurous and boiling, a giant clenched fist of smoke brandished at the heavens from the fuming earth below. A red bracelet of fire glowed at the wrist and then disappeared. Beneath it, stretching right down to the ground, was a revolving column of yellow smoke, fanning out at the bottom to a dark pyramid, wider at its base than at the top. The darkness of the pyramid was due to a dust being sucked up by the heat . It reminded Tibbetts of a boiling pot of tar, black and boiling underneath with a steam haze on top of it. Blue and red flames leaped in all directions, followed by dreadful thunder and unbearable waves of heat which cut down the citizens as they fell. In addition, a gaseous wave, travelling at high speed, carried gamma radiation across a distance of four miles.

This is what the crew on board the *Enola Gay* reported:

We watched a giant pillar of purple fire, 10 000 feet high, shoot up like a meteor coming from the earth instead of outer space. It was no longer smoke, or dust, or even a cloud of fire. It was a living thing, a new species of being, born before our incredulous eyes. Even as we watched, a ground mushroom came shooting out of the top to 45 000 feet, a mushroom top that was even more alive than the pillar, seething and boiling in a white fury of creamy foam, a thousand geysers rolled into one. It kept struggling in elemental fury, like a creature in the act of breaking the bonds that held it down. When we last saw it, it had changed into a flower-like form, its giant petals curving downwards, creamy-white outside, rose-coloured inside. The boiling pillar had become a giant mountain of jumbled rainbows. Much living substance had gone into those rainbows.*

Captain Robert Lewis, *Enola Gay*'s co-pilot, looking down from thousands of feet, murmured aloud, 'My God, what have we done?' The scene was reminiscent of the Day of the Lord described in the Bible in the second letter of St Peter (*2 Peter 3: 8-14*): 'The Day of the Lord will come like a thief, and then with a roar the sky will vanish, the elements will catch fire and fall apart, the earth and all that it contains will be burnt up.' Was this the Day of the Lord 'when the sky will dissolve in flames and the elements melt in the heat?'

It was for over 100 000 men, women and children – in the batting of an eyelid.

---

* William L. Lawrence, *Dawn over Zero*, Knopf, New York 1946 (quoted in L.Cheshire, *The Light of Many Suns*. 58–9).

Chapter Six

Pika-Don: Nobori-Cho

The magazine Father Kleinsorge was reading flew from his hands when a tremendous flash of light – as if some monstrous photographer's flashbulb had exploded in his face – blinded him. Everything turned white, whiter than any white he had ever seen. He flung his hands to his eyes. A blast of hot air burnt his cheeks, as if the door to Hell had been opened. The very air seemed to catch alight. A pressure wave flung him backwards. The splinters and shards of glass and fragments of tile enveloped him. He heard no roar – almost no one in Hiroshima recalls hearing any noise of the bomb. But a fisherman in his sampan in the Inland Sea, near Tsuzu, twenty miles away, saw the flash and heard a tremendous explosion, 'that vibrated to the pit of [his] stomach'. The thunder was much greater than when the B-29s bombed Iwakuni, only five miles away.

What had happened, wondered Father Kleinsorge? What Armageddon had belched out of the peaceful summer's sky? Had a meteor collided with the earth, as he read about as a boy? Was it a direct hit from a bomb? Had the Ujina ammunition depot exploded? Was this the end of the world? For a few seconds he was out of his mind. He didn't know how he got out of the house. The next thing he was conscious of was that he was wandering around in the Mission's vegetable plot in his underpants. He put his hand to his left side; the palm was red with blood. The only building standing in the whole of Nobori-cho was the Mission House, which had long before been braced and double-braced by Brother Gropper, who was terrified of earthquakes – he still remembered the earthquake of 1923. The rest was a desert landscape, mounds of collapsed buildings in an endless plain of rubble and cinders. It was as if some giant had swept his hand across the landscape, the buildings crumbling like a pack of cards. Everything was flattened. Even the Castle had disappeared. He could see all the way across the levelled city to the sea coast far away. The island between the Honkaya and the Motoyasu branches of the River Ohta lay like a skinned turkey hanging by its beak from the Aioi Bridge. The only buildings standing were a few modern ones built of steel and reinforced concrete, like the modern Chamber of Commerce Building and the Fukuya Department Store. Even the Museum of Science and Industry was shorn to its steel skeleton. These stood like tombstones in a vast fire-swept cemetery.

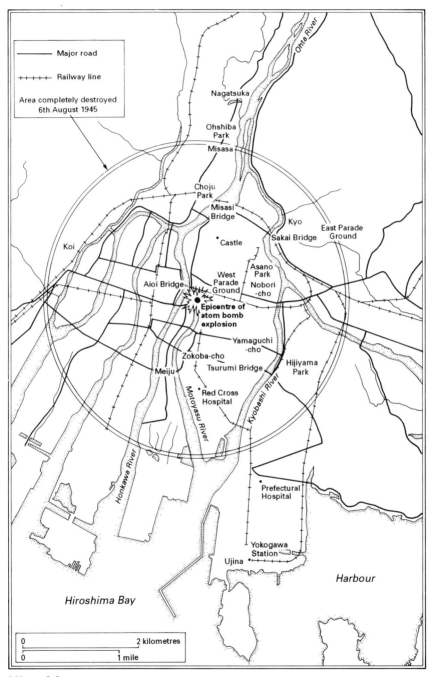

Hiroshima

Over what had been the city of Hiroshima a few minutes earlier, an immense white thundercloud was rising, as large as the city itself. The top of the cloud turned and twisted, flashing vermilion flame in all directions. Now the cloud hovered over the entire basin of the Ohta River. Under what seemed a local dust cloud, the day grew darker and darker into a twilight. He stared at the darkening sky. 'Why is it night already?' he wondered to himself. Then it started to rain, big, black and purple globules, the result of vaporisation of moisture in the fireball and subsequent condensation. Then the black rain stopped abruptly.

He heard a voice crying out, over and over, 'Shu Jesusu, awaremi tamai! Our Lord Jesus, have pity on us.' It was Mrs Murata, the housekeeper. Out of the darkness Father Superior La Salle appeared round the corner of the building. He was covered in blood. As the flash had struck he had twisted away from the window; long shards of broken glass had embedded themselves into his exposed back and lower extremities. He had a deep gash in his left leg.

Two further figures appeared. It was Father Cieslik supporting Father Schiffer, who was covered with blood, spurting out like red ink from a water pistol from a cut above his left ear. Father Schiffer was as white as a sheet. He had been sitting in his room in the Parish House when the bomb had struck. The House collapsed and he was buried under a wall. The church, the school and nearby buildings had all collapsed at once. As he lay trapped under the wall he could hear the screams of children crying for help, trapped under the ruins of the school building. They were eventually rescued after a great deal of effort. There were no bandages, so, to stop the profuse bleeding, and having nothing better to hand, they wrapped Father Schiffer's head in newspapers and a shirt, so that he looked like a turbaned merchant from the Orient.

Father Cieslik seemed unhurt. After the flash he had dived into a doorway which he had previously reckoned to be the safest place inside the building, and when the blast came he was not injured. Father La Salle asked Father Cieslik to take Father Schiffer to a doctor before he bled to death, and suggested either Dr Kanda, who lived on the next corner, or Dr Fujii, about six blocks away. The two men went out of the compound and up where once the street had been.

An hysterical woman rushed up to Father Kleinsorge. She was the daughter of Mr Hoshijima, the mission catechist. She screamed that her mother and sister were buried under the ruins of their house, which was at the back of the Jesuit compound. At the same time the priests noticed that the house of the kindergarten teacher at the front of the compound had collapsed on her. While Father La Salle, his back still pierced with glass, with the help of Mrs Murata dug the teacher out, Father Kleinsorge went to the catechist's fallen house and began lifting things off the top of the pile. There was not a sound underneath; he was sure the Hoshijima women had been killed. At last, under what had been a corner of the kitchen, he saw Mrs Hoshijima's head. Believing her dead, he began to haul her out by the hair, but suddenly she screamed, '*Itai! Itai!* (It hurts! It hurts!).' He dug some more and lifted her out. He managed, too, to find her daughter in the rubble and free her. Neither was too badly hurt.

By now the fires were scorching the heavens; it looked like a sunset sky. The crackling and sizzling of the burning timbers was disturbed every now and then by thunderous explosions, as if drums of gasoline were blowing up. There were flames everywhere. But there was no one to extinguish them. Even if any fire stations had survived, they would have been useless since the city's water mains, split open, could provide no pressure. All water and electricity was cut off. The whole area was one fantastic bonfire.

A public bath next door to the Mission House had caught fire, but since the wind was southerly, the priests thought their wooden house would be spared. Nevertheless, as a precaution, Father Kleinsorge went inside to fetch some things he wanted to save. He found his room in a state of total and illogical confusion. A first-aid kit was hanging undisturbed on a hook on the wall, but his clothes, which had been on other hooks nearby, were nowhere to be seen. His desk was in splinters all over the room. But a mere papier-maché suitcase, which he had kept under the desk, stood with its handle up, and without a scratch on it, in the doorway of the room, where he could not miss it. (He later came to regard this as a bit of Providential interference, since the suitcase contained his breviary, the account books for the whole diocese, and a considerable amount of paper money belonging to the Mission, for which he was responsible.) He ran out of the house and deposited the suitcase in the mission *kura*, a separate fire-proof building made of stone or plaster with thick walls and small windows, used for storing valuables.

At about this time, Father Cieslik and Father Schiffer, who was still spurting blood, came back and said that Dr Kanda's house had been demolished and that raging fires prevented them from getting to Dr Fujii's private hospital, on the bank of the Kyo River. Father Kleinsorge stemmed Father Schiffer's spurting cut as well as he could with some bandage that Dr Fujii had given the priests a few days before. When he finished, he ran back into the Mission House and found the jacket of his military uniform and an old pair of grey trousers. He put them on and went outside. A woman from next door ran up to him and shouted that her husband was buried under her house and the house was on fire; Father Kleinsorge must come and save him.

'Do you know exactly which part of the house he is under?' he asked.

'Yes, yes,' she replied. 'Come quickly.'

They went around to the house, the remains of which blazed violently, but when they got there, it turned out that the woman had no idea where her husband was. Father Kleinsorge shouted several times, 'Is anyone there?' There was no answer. Father Kleinsorge said to the woman, 'We must get away or we will all die.'

The fires raged in every direction. Houses all around were burning funeral pyres. (The wind had now swung around and was from the north.) The oncoming flames had reached them. It was time to flee for their lives. Just then the kindergarten teacher pointed out to the priests Mr Fukai, the secretary of the mission, who was standing at his window on the second floor of the Mission House, facing in the direction of the explosion, weeping. Father Cieslik thought the stairs unusable, so he ran around to the back of the Mission House to look for a ladder. There he heard people crying for help under a nearby fallen roof. He called passers-by running away in the street to help him lift it, but nobody paid any attention, and he had to leave the buried ones to die. Father Kleinsorge ran inside the house and scrambled up the stairs, littered with splinters, tiles, jagged pieces of glass, plaster and lathing. He called to Mr Fukai from the doorway of his room.

Mr Fukai was completely uninjured. The short, middle-aged man turned around slowly and said 'Leave me here.' He had a queer, almost mesmerized expression on his face. In fact, he was completely out of his mind. He refused to leave, saying that he didn't want to survive the destruction of his fatherland.

Father Kleinsorge went into the room and took the secretary by the collar of his coat and said, 'Come with me or you'll die.'

Again Mr Fukai protested, 'Leave me here to die.'

Father Kleinsorge began to shove and haul Mr Fukai out of the room. Then Mr Takemoto, a theology student, came up and grabbed Mr Fukai's feet, while Father Kleinsorge took his shoulders, and together they carried him downstairs and outdoors.

'I can't walk!' Mr Fukai cried. 'Leave me here!'

Father Kleinsorge got his paper suitcase with the papers and money in it and took up Mr Fukai pickaback, and the party started for the East Parade Ground, their district's evacuation area. As they went out of the gate, Mr Fukai, quite hysterical now, kept beating on Father Kleinsorge's shoulders, shouting, 'I won't leave. I won't leave.'

The three willow trees by the entrance, erect and green a few minutes ago, now stood with bowed heads; they had given up the fight. The cherry trees, too, were charred, black sentinels.

The streets were cluttered with parts of houses and stores that had slid into them. They clambered over the hot, smoking roofs, their occupants pinned under their buildings and buried alive. From every second or third house came the screams of people trapped and abandoned, pleading for help. But even in their agony they never lost their politeness. '*Tasukete kure!* (Help if you please)!' they cried.

Occasionally the cries for help in Japanese were broken by those in Korean – '*Aigoh! Aigoh!* (God help me!)'. The Koreans were employed mainly in the Gunzoku Labour Battalions. Like the Chinese immigrants, they were regarded as second class citizens.

The priests recognized several of the ruins from which the cries for help were coming. But the flames were already there, it was too late for help. A young man came running towards them, half crazed and calling for help. For twenty minutes he had been hearing his mother's voice as she lay buried under the rubble of what had been their home. But the flames were by now already enveloping her body and his efforts to lift the large wooden beams that held her captive were in vain.

Mr Fukai was proving an immense weight on Father Kleinsorge's back. All the time he kept pleading, 'Let me stay.'

They joined the ranks of the walking dead. Those who could run or walk or hobble or even drag themselves on the ground, were fleeing in terror, out of flattened houses, offices, schoolrooms, public places, factories. They knew not where; they were fleeing the flames. They were all dyed red with blood. Secretaries, their black hair flying loose – those who still had any hair – their normally spotless white blouses stained with blood and filth, skipped along as fast as they could. A little child, his burnt face swollen like a balloon, was crying out for its mother. One secretary, stripped naked by the blast with only her sandals and a first-aid kit hanging from her shoulder, stopped to help. In no time at all the stampeding crowd following behind had trampled her – and the child. Neither were seen again.

A woman, her body all greasy and purple like an egg-plant, all covered with blood, her hair red brown and frizzled, ran past, calling out her child's name '*Hanako-chan! Hanako-chan!*' A mother lay face downward tightly holding her dead baby with one arm and groaning pitifully. Children were calling the names of their fathers and mothers and brothers and sisters. The cries '*kaa-chan*' (mummy) and '*too-chan*' (daddy) were everywhere. A man shouting '*Shinzi! Shinzi!*' limped past, calling for his lost child. Another man, sitting by the roadside, pressing together with both hands a gaping red wound, like a burst pomegranate, that had been gouged out of his leg by glass, was crying out the names of his wife and children. A young schoolgirl, miraculously unscarred, and still in her uniform, was leading her father and mother, completely naked, by the hand. An old man, the skin from his face and body peeling off like a potato skin, was mumbling his prayers as his faltering steps tried to keep up with the frenzied crowd. The wounded supported the maimed; disfigured families huddled together. One teacher, her hair turned white, was clutching her students close to her like a mother hen protecting her baby chicks, all paralysed with terror. Those who had lost the strength to keep moving just sat by the roadside, vomited and waited for death. The motionless ones were the lucky ones – they were already dead.

The sight of those badly burned by the hot breath of the atomic blast was beyond imagination. Some had been burned to a cinder standing up. Others had literally been roasted alive. Those who survived were wrapped in what looked like wisps of smoke – but the smoke was their skin – peeling off from their bodies in red strips. They looked like so many cadavers emerged from their graves. They were all stark naked or in tattered shreds of clothing. Their skin, rust-coloured from burns and blood, hung from their faces and hands, from their limbs and bodies, like rags. The skin of their hands were torn away at the wrists, and hung from their fingernails looking like gloves turned inside out. You couldn't tell the men from the women. Some held their arms up, their fingers webbed, as if in supplication, to keep the dangling flesh from brushing into their sides. Others had their arms up as they were caught shading their eyes from the sun while looking up at the parachutes floating down. Others walked with their hair and eyebrows burned off. All looked like bloated balloons. Many had their eyes so swollen that they couldn't see and were staggering around like blind people, groups of them colliding with each other and falling down. Some men had patterns on their burnt skins where their braces had absorbed the heat from the bomb and conducted it to their skins. Women had patterns of flowers on their bodies where their white skins had repelled the heat which the flowers on their kimonos had absorbed. Everywhere came the pleas for water.

'*Mizu, mizu*; find me water please.' People whose faces were bloated or burnt beyond recognition were begging for water. Someone shouted: 'No, don't give him water. He'll die if you give him water.' (It was believed that fluids were dangerous to burn patients.) People were drinking even the filthy water by the wayside.

Those too injured to move begged, 'Please pour water on me.' People who could no longer bear the heat jumped into water tanks to quench their thirst and burns – every household had been ordered to build a water-tank as a precaution in the event of air-raids. But even here the water was hot. In one tank a mother was weeping, holding above her head a naked baby that was burned bright red all over its body. Another mother was crying and sobbing as she gave her burned breasts to her baby. In another tank some school-children stood with only their heads above water, clasping their two hands together as they implored for help or cried for their parents. But everyone who passed was wounded, all of them, and unable to help.

Fallen telephone poles were everywhere, their wires lying like so many dead, but red-hot, snakes, wrapping themselves around ankles. So, too, were the snapped electric wires, some still live, jumbled on the ground like a barbed wire entanglement. The stump of a telephone pole was still smouldering. A horse that had been tethered to a telephone pole was rearing wildly, all covered in blood. Another horse, naked and hairless, its skull encrusted with blood, had lost its eyes: it kept colliding with objects and then would stumble on, with sunken head, its flaring, puffing, nostrils searching for a stable that was no longer there. Inadvertently it kept treading on the dead and injured lying by the roadside. Further on a soldier and his horse lay dead together. Near them a mother and her baby also lay dead together.

The gruesome procession moved on, heads bowed, looking straight ahead with expressionless faces – those that still had recognizable faces. There were no handcarts or peasants' wagons or prams – they had all been incinerated. Bicycles had been turned into corkscrews; they lay crumpled in the streets. A section of a car engine had the fused skeleton of the mechanic who had been tinkering with it. A blackened sewing-machine would no longer provide her meagre income for one industrious housewife. The charred shells of streetcars, halted in mid motion, stood on melted rails, the passengers inside all burnt to cinders. Sometimes their path was blocked by whole walls of dead and dying people. They crept between and around them as best they could. There were cries of '*Zuru, zuru*', as the flesh from a corpse's body stuck to the hand that was moving it aside to make way. The bones creaked and cracked under the fleeing feet.

Their path was suddenly blocked. The whole street was aflame with a block of fallen houses. The crowd detoured to the right. They made for Sakai Bridge which would take them across the Kyobashi River to the East Parade Ground, the designated evacuation area for their neighbourhood. The crush of hysterical human beings had pushed out the iron railings, catapulting hundreds to death by drowning. Many made no move to save themselves. Others, yelling 'Hot! Hot!' jumped into the water, and since they could not move their limbs freely, perished. A young girl jumped in, screaming 'I want to die quickly.' The river was not a stream of flowing water but rather a stream of drifting dead bodies, moving downstream on the muddy current to meet the lapping tides of the Inland Seto Sea. The corpses, some with their skin dangling like strands of dark sea-weed, floated down like the *kimekoni* paper dolls that floated on the Kyobashi on New Year's Day, carrying everyone's troubles to the sea.

Across the river the sight was even more harrowing. A whole community of people was a sheet of fire. You could smell the burning flesh. Horses, threatened by the fire, were whinnying as they tugged on their halters.

The priests decided to take refuge in Asano Park, off to their left, near the Castle. It was a private estate belonging to the wealthy Asano family, who owned the Toyo Kisen Kaisha Steamship line. As they neared the Park it looked as if the Castle had suffered a direct hit. There was nothing left of it. The carp floated belly up in the moat. There was nothing left either of the Gokoku Shrine alongside the garrison parade ground. They straggled past the ruins. A detachment of soldiers from the Second Western Regiment was there. All dead; but still drawn up with military precision. At their head, his uniform tunic still recognizable, was their officer. He still held his drawn sword in his hand, but the whole lower part of his body was...white bones. Emerging from Hijiyama Hill, the only rising land formation to break Hiroshima's uniformly flat terrain, was a troop of soldiers, covered all over in blood, silent and dazed. They had been burrowing into the sacred hillside – making one of thousands of dug-outs in which the Japanese intended to resist the invasion, hill by hill, life for life.

They passed the French military cemetery. Many of the crosses commemorating the soldiers who had died of yellow fever at the time of the Boxer Rebellion in 1900 were now lying horizontal, on the flat, horizontal slabs. All through the present war, even though the French were enemies of Japan, a group of Japanese women had carefully tended the graves. Between the graves were carefully placed beer and *sake* bottles and plates of ossified food. The Japanese had a special respect for the graves of warriors.

Father Kleinsorge, who had been weakened by his bad case of diarrhoea, began to stagger under his protesting load and as he tried to climb up over the wreckage of several houses that blocked their way to the Park, he stumbled, dropped Mr Fukai, and plunged down, head over heels, to the sandy bank of the river. When he picked himself up, he saw Mr Fukai running away. He shouted to a dozen soldiers, who were standing by the bridge, to stop Mr Fukai. But they seemed as dazed and bewildered as everybody else. Mr Fukai got away from them and the last they saw of the small, broken man, was of him running back toward the inferno.

The river, no longer shimmering green with the reflected glint of polished bronze, was crowded with people, some standing, some crouching, some lying in the shallows, taking refuge in the cool water. Some people tottered to the edge of the river, fell in and were drowned. It was ebb tide, so the water in the channel was low, but flowing swiftly to the sea. A young girl, horribly burned, in her underwear, had strayed out too deep. She held out her hand but her skin just peeled off as someone grabbed at her arm. People were carrying water from the river – but that was a mistake since it was tidal and brackish. Bloated bodies floated and bobbled around. People just brushed them aside and drank. Those who quenched their thirst from the river were nauseated and soon began vomiting. Others were nauseated, too; but they thought that was because of the gas given off by the bomb. There was a strong odour of ionization, an 'electric smell', caused by the bomb's fission.

No one knew what had caused the disaster. Some thought it had been a Molotoffano *hamakago* – a Molotov 'flower or bread-basket', scattering clusters of bombs instead. Others hazarded that fine magnesium powder had been sprayed over the city by a single plane, and the powder exploded when it came into contact with the live electric wires of the city's power station.

The Park was like a battle-field, with rank on rank of dead and injured and burned and bleeding lying everywhere, their red-black faces staring wildly. It was hard to distinguish the living from the dead, for most of the people lay still, their eyes open. People poured into the Park. As it had been far enough away from the explosion its bamboos, pines, laurel, and maples were still alive, and the green place invited refugees – partly because they believed that if the Americans came back, they would bomb only buildings; partly because the foliage seemed a centre of coolness and life, and the estate's exquisitely precise rock gardens, with their quiet pools and arching bridges, were very Japanese, homely, secure; and also partly because of an irresistible, atavistic urge to hide under leaves. A girl, her hair burned off, and quite naked, was taking cover. Only the rubber belt that had held up her trousers still hung round her hips. Another, her hair all singed, stood in rags that smoked as if they were about to burst into flame. A military policeman, leaning on his sword, cried aloud as he stroked the half-burned head of a girl, only the elastic of her *mompe* left unburnt. Another policeman, with utmost patience, was trying to feed moistened bread to a small child whose mother had collapsed on the roadside.

Understandably, many people had become insane. One man, severely burned and in tatters, walked up and down proclaiming 'I am a General of the Army'. Maybe he was. Another man, brandishing a flag, was shouting *'Banzai! Banzai!'*

The priests exchanged greetings with the injured and the dying and finally settled down in a bamboo grove by the river bank. To Father Kleinsorge, a Westerner, the silence in the grove by the river, where hundreds of gruesomely wounded suffered together, was one of the most dreadful and awesome experiences of his whole life. The hurt ones were quiet; no one wept, much less screamed in pain; no one complained; none of the many who died did so noisily; not even the children cried; very few people even spoke. And when Father Kleinsorge gave water to some whose faces had been almost blotted out by flash burns, they took their share and then raised themselves a little and bowed to him, in thanks. *'Arigato gozaimashita'*! (Thank you very much!)' they would say. Some could barely open their lips, the precious drops spilling down their grilled chins.

Father La Salle lay down and went right to sleep. Mr Takemoto, the theological student, who was wearing slippers, had carried with him a bundle of clothes, in which he had packed two pairs of leather shoes. When he sat down with the others, he found that the bundle had broken open and a couple of shoes had fallen out and now he had only two lefts. He retraced his steps and found one right.

When he rejoined the priests, he said, 'It's funny, but things don't matter any more. Yesterday, my shoes were my most important possessions. Today, I don't care. One pair is enough.'

Father Cieslik said, 'I know. I started to bring my books along, and then I thought, this is no time for books.'

A man nearby was so badly burned they couldn't tell whether he was young or old. They put a blanket down for him and a pillow. While they looked at him he swelled up to three times his size and his whole body got soft and turned the colour of dirt.

'Water, water,' he kept pleading in a faint voice.

Flies began to crawl over him. An awful smell came from his body. People ran past if they came too near. All day a thick, noxious miasma had hung over Hiroshima, clogging nostrils and throats and burning into the cranial cavities. But even that poisonous gas and smell were many times preferable to this.

As the hours passed the direct exposure to the sun turned up the heat of many burns. A heavy pall of black and yellow smoke continued to hang over everything. Early in the afternoon the fires reached the woods of Asano Park. Father Kleinsorge moved Father Schiffer and Father La Salle close to the river bank, in the hope of getting across the river if the fires approached too near. Meanwhile Mr Tanimoto, the Methodist pastor, who had been doing sterling work in ferrying the wounded across the river single-handedly, using a punt he had procured from somewhere, organised a group of volunteers to help fight the advancing fires. Those of the priests who could joined the volunteers. Some people were sent to look for buckets and basins, others began beating the burning underbrush with their clothes, others used any utensils to hand to form a bucket chain from one of the pools in the rock gardens. Meanwhile the people in the Park were becoming more and more frightened and began to push those unfortunates who were on the river bank into the water, and several were drowned. For more than two hours the volunteers struggled with the fires. Finally, the flames succumbed.

When Father Kleinsorge got back after fighting the flames, he found Father Schiffer still bleeding and terribly pale. Some Japanese stood around, staring at him.

Father Schiffer whispered, with a weak smile, 'It is as if I were already dead.'

'Not yet,' said Father Kleinsorge. He had brought Dr Fujii's first-aid kit with him, and he had noticed Dr Kanda in the crowd, so he sought him out and asked him if he would dress Father Schiffer's bad cuts. Dr Kanda had seen his wife and daughter dead in the ruins of his hospital; he sat now with his head in his hands.

'I can't do anything,' he said.

Father Kleinsorge bound more bandage around Father Schiffer's head, moved him into a steep place and settled him so that his head was high. Soon the bleeding diminished.

There was a roar of approaching aeroplanes. Someone shouted 'They're coming to strafe us.' Many people, including the badly burned ones, crawled into the bushes and stayed there until the drone, evidently of a reconnaissance or weather plane, died away. It began to rain. The drops were huge, the size of marbles, and black as ink. The rain, like the world, was black.

Someone shouted, 'The Americans are dropping gasoline. They are going to set fire to us.' Some people had come to believe that so much of Hiroshima had been devastated by fire because a single American plane had sprayed gasoline on the city and then set fire to it. But the drops were water. They were drops of condensed moisture falling from the tower of dust, heat and fission fragments that had been drawn high into the sky above Hiroshima.

The black rain did little to put out the fires but it helped further to frighten and confuse an already terrified people. Accompanying the black raindrops, which hurt as if being pelted with stones, hot sparks began to fall from the grey sky like a sudden shower. The sparks were like big chunks of fire falling as rain.

Then came a wind, a whirlwind. The elements had gone mad. There had been no wind early on. But now brisk winds were blowing every which way. This was the fire wind blasting back to earth, accelerating as the temperature of the air above the city rose because of the fires. In no time at all oppressive blasts of hot air and the showers of cinders made it impossible to stand. The spiralling vortex sucked up everything. Huge trees were uprooted and lifted up like leaves into the air. Iron roofing, *tsubo* mats, doors, papers, were sucked up. The only way not to become airborne was to lie flat on the ground. The vortex moved out on to the river causing a huge water spout, spraying water one hundred metres high. Those refugees not strong enough were blown into the angry waters.

When the storm abated Mr Tanimoto resumed ferrying people across the river. Father Kleinsorge asked the theological student to go across and make his way out to the Jesuit Novitiate at Nagatsuka, about three miles from the centre of town, and to request the priests there to come with help for Fathers Schiffer and La Salle. Mr Takemoto got into Mr Tanimoto's boat and went off with him. The Methodist pastor used a thick bamboo pole for propulsion. In the centre of the river, however, it was too deep to pole the punt across and it had to be paddled with the bare hands.

Late in the afternoon people were getting hungry and begging for food. When Mr Tanimoto returned, he and Father Kleinsorge decided to go back into the city to get some rice from Mr Tanimoto's *tonari-gumi* (Neighbourhood Association) air-raid shelter and from the Mission shelter. Father Cieslik and two or three others went with them. They soon got lost. They could not work out where they were. A few hours earlier there had been a city of 245 000 now it was a pile of rubble, with range upon range of collapsed buildings. They picked out one or two buildings that happened to be standing. There was the Exhibition Building, with its smashed dome, the Museum of Science and Industry, and the Chamber of Commerce Building, the Fukuya Department Store, still sizzling and crackling. These few, gutted, buildings, still standing, accentuated the horizontality of everything else. A black pillar of cloud still billowed upward.

They followed the twisted and tangled tracks of streetcars, still burning hot and dangerous, to help give them their bearings. Pieces of paper and cloth were caught on electric wires, severed and dangling dangerously. The asphalt on the streets was still soft from the heat; walking was difficult. They passed thousands of dead. Charred people, burned black, lay where they had been cut down by the blast, vacant eyes staring wide open. It was like the sight that must have greeted the excavators of the ashen cemetery that had once been in Pompeii, the dead in the postures of their flight. A baby, its cute little hands clenched tight, lay, its eyes closed. They passed only one live woman, her hair frizzled up and covered in dust, her skin roasted.

'My husband is in those ashes,' she cried, pointing. A withered spray of flowers lay on a roof tile beside the head of a corpse lying in the road. The smell was like too-hot electric hair-curlers. It was the smell of burned flesh and burned hair. It was the smell of death.

Their hearts dropped with sadness when they saw that the Mission House, the only erect building in Nobori-cho, had gone up in a lick of flame. In the garden, on the way to the shelter, they noticed a pumpkin roasted on the vine. They tasted it and it was good. They retrieved several bags of rice and gathered up several other cooked pumpkins, along with some potatoes that had baked nicely under the ground and started back to Asano Park.

That evening, as the Gotterdämmerung sun was slowly sinking into a plume of purple smoke rising over Hiroshima, passing through all the different discolourations of a deep bruise, a naval launch sailed up the river, dodging floating corpses as best it could. It stopped opposite the Park. A young naval officer stood up in the launch and shouted through a megaphone,

'Be patient! A naval hospital ship is coming to take care of you!'

The sight of the shipshape launch against a background of the havoc across the river; the unruffled young man in his neat uniform; above all, the promise of medical help – the first word of possible succour anyone had heard in nearly twelve awful hours – cheered the people in the park tremendously.

Despite the gnats and mosquitoes and the flies that settled without discrimination on the living and the dead, sheer exhaustion brought merciful sleep to some of the group; and the darkness kindly hid the gruesome forms – but not the terrible smell – of those lying about on the ground. Against the pink glow of the burned city it was hard to pick out the lights of the fishing boats in the distance of Hiroshima Bay.

Chapter Seven

Pika-Don: Nagatsuka

It was about four o'clock in the afternoon when Mr Takemoto, the theology student, reached the Jesuit Novitiate at Nagatsuka. He found that here, too, the bomb had wreaked destruction, although nothing on the scale he had seen in the centre of the city.

That morning Father Arrupe had entered his study at 8.10 a.m. On the wall in front of his desk was a crucifix and a timepiece. He still had some minutes before his first class.

But he didn't. For at that instant a blinding light, like burning magnesium, dazzling as a bolt of lightning, filled the entire room. There was no sound. Everything seemed to stop: the world seemed to be in a state of suspense. Was this the holocaust, the end of the world? he wondered. From his studies of Comparative Religion as a young novice he was reminded of the words in the Sanskrit *Bhagavad Gita*. 'If the radiance of a thousand suns were to burst into the sky, that would be like the splendour of the Mighty One.'

It was the Feast of the Transfiguration of Our Lord. That very morning at Mass he had read Matthew's account.

Jesus took with him Peter, James and John and led them up a high mountain. There he was transfigured before them. His face shone like the sun, and his clothes became as white as the light ...

Then a bright cloud enveloped them, and a voice from the cloud said, 'This is my Son, whom I love; with him I am well pleased. Listen to Him!'

When the disciples heard this, they fell face down to the ground, terrified. But Jesus came and touched them.

'Get up,' He said. 'Don't be afraid.'*

Arrupe jumped up to see what was happening. As he opened the door which faced the city a tremendous explosion shattered his eardrums. A blast of hot air sent him crashing to the other side of the room where he collapsed to the floor. Bits of glass, roof tiles and bricks rained down on him. A large fragment of glass miraculously missed him and buried itself into the wall opposite. The *tatami* mat was buried under a foot and a half of plaster, glass and debris. There

---

* *Matthew 17:1-7*

74

was debris everywhere. It was some four or five seconds before he was able to pick himself up. These few seconds seemed an eternity – when one fears that a beam is about to crash down and flatten one's skull at any moment time is incredibly prolonged. He looked at the clock. It was still hanging in its place, but motionless. It was still ten minutes past eight. The clock pendulum seemed nailed down as if to record for posterity the time of birth of man's ultimate weapon of mass destruction.

It slowly dawned on Father Arrupe that a monster bomb must have exploded directly over the house. He rushed through the rest of the building. He had direct responsibility for thirty-five young men studying for the priesthood, many of whom had been evacuated from the Tokyo Novitiate to the comparative – until now – safety of the Hiroshima one. Sitting in the hallway was a dazed German priest, a book still in his hands. A few seconds earlier he had been resting against the window sill of his room, several yards away. The priest was no small man; he weighed over 200lbs. Everything was in a state of confusion. All the windows had been smashed and all the doors forced inwards; all the bookshelves had tumbled down and books were strewn everywhere. Some of the novices and priests were bleeding from fragments of glass, but none was seriously injured. No one seemed to have come to serious harm.

They went into the garden to see where the bomb had fallen. They stared at each other in total disbelief: there was no crater in the ground anywhere; there was no sign of an explosion. The trees and flowers were all quite fresh and normal. But it was surely a bomb. They ventured into the rice fields surrounding the House, looking for where the bomb had landed. But again there was no hole or sign of any explosion. Yet not a door or window remained in place. At least the main building still stood – another credit to the building skills of Brother Gropper.

They then looked across to the city. Dense columns of black smoke rose to the heavens; enormous flames leaped into the sky, accompanied by the sound of smaller explosions. They concluded an incendiary bomb with an especially strong explosive action had struck the city. Down in the valley, a mile away, several peasant houses were on fire and the woods on the opposite side of the valley were aflame. They climbed a hill to get a better view. They could not believe their eyes. Below them lay a city totally annihilated, a hundred thousand souls had vanished into oblivion – dead before they knew it. The city was flaming red; a huge mushroom-like cloud billowed up into the sky.

About half an hour after the explosion a procession of people, getting thicker by the minute, began to stream up the valley. They were fleeing the burning city. They were unable to run, the horrific injuries they had sustained made sure of that. Most were bleeding profusely or suffering from severe burns. Many displayed horrible wounds of the extremities and back. The less seriously injured carried the more serious victims on their backs. A group of young women, eighteen to twenty years old, clung to one another as they dragged themselves along the road. One had a blister that covered her entire chest, burns across her face and a gaping cut in her scalp, probably caused by a falling tile; blood coursed down her face.

The priests converted their beautiful chapel into a temporary hospital, taking in about fifty of the most wounded refugees. It was fortunate that Father Arrupe was a doctor. Before joining the priesthood he had studied medicine at the University of Madrid for five years. He had won prizes for anatomical studies and for therapeutics. As part of his medical studies he obtained permission to work in the Office of Verification at the Grotto in Lourdes, in the Pyrenees. The staff at the University,most of whom were atheists, scoffed at his going to such a place of superstition. At the Office of Verification, too, the doctors were all atheists. Much to his amazement he was actually present when, not one, but three miraculous cures occurred in front of his own eyes. It was these experiences that led him to give up his medical studies and join the novitiate of the Society of Jesus at Loyola. As he later recalled, 'I felt that God was calling me not only to cure bodies but also to cure souls.' That was in 1927, when Pedro Arrupe was twenty years old.

Father Arrupe rushed into the house to rescue any medical supplies. He found a medical chest under some rubble. He was able to retrieve some iodine, some aspirin tablets and some bicarbonate of soda. These were the only medicaments available to hundreds crying out desperately for medical help. The priests gave what first aid they could. The quantities of fat so carefully saved up during the lean years of the war were soon used up in treating the burns. Underclothing, sheets, anything at hand, were torn up to make bandages. Soon there were no drugs left; all they could do was clean up the wounds. Meanwhile the chapel and library and any other rooms available were cleared of broken glass and debris and used as an emergency casualty clearing station, the dying being placed on mats of straw. But very soon the makeshift hospital had reached its capacity of 150 'beds'. It couldn't take any more. The other unfortunates had to lie down in the garden, in the fields, in the road – wherever they could find space.

The wounded – those who could utter any sounds – kept muttering the words *'pika-don'*. *Pika-Don* (flash-bang; lightning-thunder) was their name for the devastating bomb.

In addition to medicine, what the injured needed was food to provide the energy required to combat the haemorrhages, fever and infection caused by the severe burns. On foot or on bicycles the young people of the House scoured the outskirts of Hiroshima to procure the life-saving food. Without wondering how, or from where, these young came back with more fish, meat, eggs and butter than had been seen in four years. Many carefully-tended gardens were sadly depleted in squashes and potatoes! This food provided the sustenance to fight the anaemia and leukemia that would develop in the majority of those exposed to atomic radiation.

In this they were emulating what the first Jesuits had done. When famine struck Rome in the winter of 1538 Ignatius and his nine companions gave themselves totally to the relief of the poor and destitute. From early dawn they would set out to beg for bread, wood, and straw to lie on; then they would carry it on their shoulders to their poor apartments. Going out again, they would gather the beggars and starving people, who literally lay in the slush of the streets of Rome, bring them together, and make them comfortable as best they could – some 400 of them at a time – or offer them some ration of food. They were thus able to help more than 3000 persons in the city.

This was not the first time Father Arrupe had experienced divine providence, either. In 1932 all 2540 Jesuits had been expelled from Spain by the Spanish Government. After the expulsion he had lived in a community of 350 persons who wondered every night if they would have any food the following day. But each day yielded enough.

It seemed the epicentre of the explosion had been at Yokogawa Station, two miles away. The Jesuit Mission and Parish House was there. The community at the Novitiate wondered over the fate of Father Superior La Salle and the other Fathers and parishioners there. They were also concerned about Father Kopp who had left early that morning to say Mass at the Shudoin Orphanage for children (called Konosono), run by the Sisters of the Poor on the edge of the city. There was no news of him or the Sisters. However, Father Kopp and the Sisters arrived later that afternoon. Father Kopp was bleeding profusely from the head and neck and had a large burn on his right palm. They had picked their way along the shore of the river and through the burning streets. The Orphanage, built by Brother Gropper, had withstood the first blast, but being built of wood, was unable to resist the flames and was burned to the ground, as was the entire district. There was no water available anywhere to curb the fires.

Father Stolle and Father Erlinghaven ventured down the road to the village of Nagatsuka. The road was full of refugees. They brought in the seriously injured who had fallen by the wayside to a temporary aid station at the village. There iodine was applied to the wounds, but they were left uncleaned, since no other medicaments were available. Those that had been brought in were laid on the floor and no one could give them any further care.

At about four o'clock in the afternoon Mr Takemoto arrived with two kindergarten children who lived in the Parish House in Nobori-cho. He reported that the Church, the House and all the adjoining buildings had been burned down. He reported that Father Superior La Salle and Father Schiffer has been seriously injured. They had taken refuge in Asano Park, on the river bank. They were too weak and injured to move.

At five o'clock Father Arrupe and some of his colleagues decided that despite the danger to themselves – for any foreigners would be suspected of being spies who had connived with the enemy in this air attack – they must go into Hiroshima to give what assistance they could. They hastily made two stretchers out of poles and boards, collected together some food and medicines and made for the devastated city, with Mr Takemoto showing the way. They first called in at the aid station at the village school where Father Arrupe was able to give some medical advice and assistance. The mayor of Nagatsuka was organizing the distribution of balls of white rice to the wounded. But the charnel-house smell was so strong that few were hungry.

The once-green paddy fields were now streaked with brown. All the houses still standing had their roofs off and broken doors and windows. But then the scenery changed suddenly. Everything was a brown scar; every house had been buffeted down or burned. Beside the Hazama Bridge at Nagatsuka people were so thirsty they were scooping up the filthy, coffee-coloured water, even with what remained of their shoes, to drink. Along the way there were men, women and children, dead and dying and begging for help. Frightfully burned people, the skin peeling off from the shoulders so that it hung from their finger-tips, screamed for help.

Ohshiba Park was like a battle-field, full of groaning wounded. People were rolling about in agony, even on top of the people burned too badly to move. Nearby, as if guarding them, a policeman stood, all covered with burns and stark naked, except for a few shreds of his trousers. An air-raid warden, in what remained of his black uniform, sat shell-shocked. It was not possible to pick up the burned by their arms or legs, the limbs were slippery where the skin had peeled off. There was a pitiful sight of a father with a baby that was crying and trying to find the breasts of its dead mother, the baby's face cut right in two along a line from above her left eyebrow, across her nose, to below the right side of her mouth, like a bursting melon. A mother, her blouse dyed bright red from blood, was calling for her lost child. A child of about six also covered all over with blood and holding a kitchen pot in his hand, was crying for his mother. An officer, limping, walked past, leading a group of twenty or more soldiers.

A father knelt on the ground before him and pleaded, 'My wife is caught up in there. Please rescue her.'

'*Shikata ga nai* [Too bad],' the officer replied, and limped on.

As they got nearer to where the city centre had once stood the macabre scene beggared the imagination. Before them lay a city flattened, except here and there a few concrete buildings, steel girders melted, a waste-land as far as the eye could see, not a plant or tree or house standing. Where once the city had been was now a gigantic burned-out scar. They couldn't get nearer the centre, which was still a sea of flames, burning with a frightful roaring sound, as though gunpowder had caught fire.

It was difficult to make any headway against the fleeing thousands. The burned and injured were calling out the names of their loved ones, of the streets where they once lived. There was often no road to walk – just the tops of roofs under which the red embers still burned. They tip-toed their way between the roof-tiles and the flames. Choju Park was littered with the dead and dying. They tip-toed over or side-stepped the prostrate forms and eventually reached the river embankment. They made their way along the river bank, between the burning and smoking ruins. Often they were forced by the heat and smoke at the level of the street to wade waist-high into the river itself.

At Misasa Bridge they came upon a long line of soldiers slowly making their way from the Chukogu Regional Army Headquarters. They were all horribly burned, and supported themselves with staves or leaned on one another. Maimed horses, their flanks all burned, stood woe-begone on the bridge, their heads hung low in bewilderment.

Soon the sky took on a deep orange colour, like twilight. Buildings were still burning, flaming red against a background of darkness. The raging fires provided enough light for them to pick their way through the burnt-out houses, roofs and tiles – and corpses. The moon, a red lantern, helped light up the way. Every now and then blue-green balls of fire would appear, like fire-flies.

Eventually they came upon their colleagues in the far corner of Asano Park. They were lying by the river bank, completely spent. Father Schiffer was stretched out on the ground, as white as a sheet. Father Arrupe made a quick examination of his seriously injured colleagues. Father Schiffer was in a critical condition. In the rush of fleeing the approaching flames at Nobori-cho the first aid treatment applied had failed to detect another wound in his outer ear; a piece of glass had penetrated a small artery and he was bleeding to death. Using some wooden sticks and bamboo planks they improvised a stretcher. Father Schiffer groaned aloud in pain as they lay him on the sticks. With the stoicism of a true Japanese the German priest smiled at Father Arrupe and said, 'Father, will you please look at my back, I think there's something there.'

They turned him face down. By the light of a torch they saw his back was completely covered with wounds made by small pieces of glass. It was difficult to dress the wounds properly in the dark. With a razor blade Don Pedro, as Father Arrupe was known, removed more than fifty fragments.

A group of soldiers walked past. Suddenly the officer rushed back, his sword raised in the classic kendo position of attack. He had heard the group talking in a foreign language and assumed that the priests were American parachutists who were reported to have landed. He shouted demanding to know who they were. He was about to strike down Father Arrupe when one of the priests explained that they were Germans – allies of the Japanese.

The priests discussed how to get Father Schiffer and Father La Salle out to the Novitiate. They were afraid that blundering through the Park in the dark would jar them too much on wooden litters, and that the wounded men would lose too much blood. Father Kleinsorge remembered Mr Tanimoto and his boat. He called out to him on the river. When Mr Tanimoto reached the bank, he said he would be glad to take the injured priests and their bearers upstream to where they could find a clearer path. They decided Father Schiffer, the more seriously injured, should go first. They put him onto one of the stretchers and lowered it into the boat, and two of them went aboard with it. Mr Tanimoto, who had no oars, poled the punt upstream.

They carried the stretcher out of the punt and set off, with Mr Takemoto, the theology student, leading the way to warn of obstacles and hazards. There were plenty of these – fallen trees, beams, fragments of ruins, wires. In the dark it was impossible to see them. One of the stretcher-bearers got his foot entangled in some telephone

wire and tripped, bringing down the litter with him. Father Schiffer
fell off and lost consciousness. When he came to he vomited. The
bearers picked him up and continued even more warily. They would
stop every one hundred metres – to relieve the pain on Father Schiffer
and also to give the stretcher-bearers a rest. The slightest movement
caused Father Schiffer agony; he was still losing large quantities of
blood.

During one of these stops they heard the anguished calls of
someone near death. But they couldn't locate the source. They
listened carefully. Someone said, 'It's underneath here somewhere.'

They had stopped to rest on the ruins of a roof. Pushing the tiles to
one side they found an old lady, half her body burned. She had been
buried there all day. She had hardly a spark of life left. They removed
her from the rubble but she died as they did so.

They passed an injured man sitting alone among the hot remains.
They had seen him earlier on their way to the Park. On the Misasi
Bridge they met Father Tappe and Father Luhmer, who had come
from the Novitiate at Nagatsuka to meet them. They had just dug a
family out of the ruins of their collapsed house, some fifty yards off
the road. They had dragged out two girls and placed them by the side
of the road. The father of the family was already dead. The mother
was still trapped under heavy beams. With great effort they were
eventually able to free her. They left Father Schiffer with the two
newly arrived priests and returned to Asano Park to get Father
Superior La Salle.

Mr Tanimoto returned to the priests by the river bank at Asano
Park. He was agitated and excited. He had seen two children
standing up to their necks in the river. Would the priests help to
rescue them? A group set off and were able to rescue the two girls
who were both badly burned. They had both lost their family. They
laid them down on the bank next to Father La Salle.

Father La Salle, who was clad only in shirt and trousers, was
freezing with cold, despite the warm summer night and the heat of
the burning city. One of the priests gave up his coat, another his shirt;
they were glad to be wearing less in the oppressive heat. They loaded
Father Superior on to the punt. Father Cieslik thought he could make
it to the Novitiate on foot, so he clambered aboard with the others.
Father Kleinsorge was too exhausted by now. He decided he would
wait in the Park until the next day. He asked the men to come back
with a handcart so they could take some of the badly injured children
to the Novitiate.

Mr Tanimoto poled off again. As the boatload of priests moved
slowly upstream, they heard weak cries for help. A woman's voice

stood out especially: 'There are people here about to be drowned! Help us! The water is rising!'

The sounds came from one of the sandspits, which jutted out from the shore. Those in the punt could see, in the reflected light of the still-burning fires, a number of wounded people lying at the edge of the river, already partly covered by the flooding tide. They had waded across during low tide to avoid the heat of the burning fires. As the tide came in most of the injured were too weak and exhausted to move. They were lying on the sand watching the waters that would soon engulf them. Mr Tanimoto punted across to the other bank, where Father La Salle was taken off the boat. He then started back alone to the sandspit.

He found about twenty men and women on the sandspit. He drove the boat onto the bank and urged them to get aboard. They did not move and he realized that they were too weak to lift themselves. He reached down and took a woman by the hands, but her skin slipped off in huge, glove-like pieces. He was so sickened by this that the had to sit down for a moment. Then he got out into the water and, though a small man, lifted several of the men and women, who were naked, into his boat. Their backs and breasts were clammy, and he remembered uneasily what the great burns he had seen during the day had been like: yellow at first, then red and swollen, with the skin sloughed off, and finally, in the evening, suppurated and smelly. With the tide risen, his bamboo pole was now too short and he had to paddle most of the way across with it. One the other side, at a higher spit, he lifted the slimy living bodies out and carried them up the slope away from the tide.

The night was hot, and it seemed even hotter because of the fires against the sky, but the younger of the two girls Mr Tanimoto and the priests had rescued complained that she was cold. Father Kleinsorge covered her with his jacket. She and her older sister had been in the salt water of the river for a couple of hours before being rescued. The younger one had huge raw flash burns on her body; the salt water must have been excruciatingly painful to her. She began to shiver heavily, and again said it was cold. Father Kleinsorge borrowed a blanket from someone nearby and wrapped her up, but she shook more and more, and said again, 'I am so cold', and then she suddenly stopped shivering and was dead.

The fires of Hiroshima burned all night. The gnats and the mosquitoes bit all night. The occasional barking of mountain dogs broke the dirge of those in great pain. Meanwhile across the river, the other priests were carrying Father La Salle to the Novitiate. Scores of tiny fragments of window glass still remained embedded in his back.

The journey, on the litter constructed out of wooden boards, was for him a painful nightmare. Unable to see in the darkness the litter-bearers stumbled into a ditch. Father La Salle was thrown to the ground; the litter broke in two. They couldn't go any further. One of the priests went ahead to get a handcart from the Novitiate. But he was lucky; he soon found one beside an empty house and wheeled it back. They lifted the Father Superior into the cart and pushed him over the bumpy road the rest of the way.

They reached the Novitiate at 4.30 a.m. Father Arrupe was looking forward to some rest. He didn't get any because someone else was in his bed. He got one half hour's sleep on the floor.

Ohshiba Park, which had previously been filled with the cries of the dying and injured, was surprisingly quiet. The reason was that two-thirds of them were now dead.

In the light of dawn Mr Tanimoto looked across the river and was horrified to discover that he hadn't carried the festering, limp, bodies high enough on the sandspit. The tide had risen above where he had put them; they hadn't the strength to move and were drowned. On the green waters of the many-mouthed River Ohta, with each ebb and flow of the tide, corpses floated like autumn leaves, now upstream, now down – curiously, the male corpses floating on their backs, the females on their bellies.

Chapter Eight

Doomsday plus one

Hiroshima, 7 August 1945

August the 7th, one day after the doomsday of *Pika-Don*, was also the anniversary of the founding of the Society of Jesus – the Jesuit Order. At five in the morning Father Arrupe celebrated Mass in the chapel. The sick and burned and dying were lying all around him. He had to be careful not to touch with his feet the children so close to him. They wanted to see more closely this stranger who was wearing such odd garments and performing ceremonies they had never seen before. He was later to recall this Mass in these words.[1]

The chapel, half destroyed, was overflowing with the wounded, who were lying on the floor very near to one another, suffering terribly, twisted with pain. I began the Mass as best I could in the midst of that mass of humanity who hadn't the slightest idea what was going on at the altar: they were non-Christians who had never attended a Mass before. I can never forget the terrible feeling I experienced when I turned toward them and saw this sight from the altar. I could not move, I stayed there as if I were paralysed, my arms outstretched, contemplating this human tragedy – human science and technological progress used to destroy the human race. They were all looking at me, eyes full of agony and despair as if they were waiting for some consolation to come from the altar. What a terrible scene!

A prayer for those who had had the savage cruelty to drop the atomic bomb came spontaneously to my lips: 'Lord, pardon them for they know not what they do'; and for those lying helpless before me, twisted with pain: 'Lord, give them the faith – that they may see; give them the strength to bear their pain.'

Torrents of graces certainly poured forth from that Host and that altar. Six months later when, having been cared for, all had left our house (only two persons died),[2] many among them had been baptized and all had learned that Christian charity knows how to

---

[1] Arrupe, Pedro, SJ, *One Jesuit's Spritual Journey*.

[2] In the official aid stations and hospitals one-third to one-half of those admitted died.

understand, help, and give a consolation that surpassed all human comforting. This charity had communicated a serenity which helps one to smile in spite of pain and to forgive those who have caused us so much suffering.

Several of the priests set off from the Novitiate to give what help they could in the city and its suburbs. One pushed a handcart to bring back anyone too burned or injured to walk. One severely wounded man refused any assistance until he had first ascertained the nationality of the helpers: he suspected they might be American paratroopers. In the broad light of day they could see more clearly the extent of the devastation. Dead bodies and carcasses of horses and dogs lay around everywhere. A mother, her baby strapped to her back, had been buried in the debris of her house. Sometimes it was difficult to pass by the purple, blackened, swollen corpses without treading on them; one would hear the crunch of a shoe or boot on bones. There was plaster and dust and blood and vomit everywhere. The smell was appalling – the priests had to tie cloths over their noses.

They heard the sound of an aircraft above. No one bothered. There weren't any air-raid shelters left to go to anyway. A young child of about seven ran out from under her temporary home of board and tin roofing, looked up and shouted, 'Give me back my sister.'

In the distance, from the docks in the south to the foothills in the north, everything had been flattened into a desert of still-smouldering ash. The only building standing, far downtown, was the towering shell of the Fukuyuma Department Store, built to withstand earthquakes.

There were people about – all heads bent, searching, searching in the ruins and ashes for their relatives. Cremation of the dead and the enshrinement of their remains is a far greater moral responsibility to the Japanese than care of the living. Solitary survivors bowed low and with great dignity before some empty, burned, plot of ground in honour of those who had perished there. A man had found his wife's gold tooth and the bone of her elbow.

New fires were springing up everywhere. These were funeral pyres. Clearance squads collected – or rather scraped up – piles of corpses that they then stacked with military precision on top of timbers from gutted houses and then set fire to them. The ashes were put in envelopes, marked with names wherever possible, and then piled in stacks near the pyres. Soldiers dug big holes, poured the corpses into them, poured kerosene over the cadavers and then set alight to them. Later they would fill in the pit. Bluish flames drifted into the sky. The sickening smell of burning human flesh hung everywhere over the city. Chinese convicts, wearing blue armbands, were fishing corpses out of the river with what looked like harpoons. They hoisted them on to an iron roasting grill, as if fish to be cooked, then spitted them. A few devout persons carried straw sandals with black and white straps to place on the feet of the corpses of their loved ones before cremation. Other devout Japanese were tearfully collecting up the ashes of their burnt relatives and putting them in urns which they would cradle in their arms as they took them to where the temple once had stood. A few had made improvised coffins into which they put the bodies, along with some home-made cakes for the dead person's next life.

As the priests got nearer the city centre Hiroshima became more and more a silent graveyard, filled only with the mute protest of the ruins. Everything stank of sulphur and dead bodies. Here and there, on tiles or a pile of ashes, messages were left: 'Sister, where are you?' or 'All safe and we are at Toyosaka.' The priests went to where the Mission House had stood and retrieved some suitcases that had been stored in the air-raid shelter and also the remains of melted chalices and patens in the ashes of the chapel.

At about noon they reached Asano Park. Father Kleinsorge was busy fetching water for the wounded in a bottle and teapot he had borrowed. There was a tap outside the gate of the Park. He stepped carefully through the rock gardens and climbed over and crawled under the trunks of fallen trees. On his return he lost his way. He passed a group of soldiers, their faces wholly burned, their eyesockets hollow; fluid from their melted eyes had run down their cheeks. They could have been anti-aircraft gunners gazing upward when the bomb exploded.

Feeding the water to the seriously burned was difficult. Some had their mouths so swollen and deformed they couldn't open them. He procured a long piece of grass, drew out the end to make a drinking straw, and force-fed them that way. A brother and sister aged five and thirteen had befriended him. Their name was Kataoka. They had just set out for school when the bomb fell. They joined their mother at the evacuation station at Asano Park. The mother then decided to go home for food and clothing. They had not seen her since. The two accompanied Father Kleinsorge back to the Novitiate. They were inconsolable, sure they would never see their mother again. Father Cieslik tried to console them as best he could by playing games with them, asking them riddles such as 'what is the cleverest animal in the world?' They would guess 'an ape', 'an elephant' and so on.

'No. It's a hippo!' came the answer, because in Japanese a hippopotamus is *kaba* which is the reverse of *baka*, meaning 'stupid'. Or he would entertain them with *kami-shibai*, story-shows making funny drawings on paper and imitating the noises of animals. Several days later the children were reconciled with their mother as a result of messages left on a board in Ujina Post Office.

By now the Novitiate had been transformed into an emergency hospital. The former University of Madrid medical student, Don Pedro Arrupe, was now priest-turned-doctor. Since the early morning Mass he had begun treating the sick and injured and burned and mentally confused and despairing, who lay everywhere – in the chapel, in the corridors, in the garden. Father Arrupe had no medicines or equipment, no anaesthetics. Not even *narucopon*, the Japanese sedative. He used his desk as an operating table, to remedy the deadly surgery the explosion had performed. His assistants tore up underwear and shirts and sheets to make bandages.

One young boy had a piece of glass, shaped like a fish-tail stuck into the pupil of his left eye. His fellow priests and students held the boy's head while Father Arrupe removed the glass without causing more damage. The little fellow was begging Don Pedro to stop.

'*Gambari! Gambari!* [Be brave],' the priest doctor kept saying. Just then there was a blinding flash, as a gas storage tank went up. The boy didn't blink. He was blind.

A man had a shard of glass sticking into his back. He had ripped his bare hands trying to extract the glass stiletto. A child, with a large wooden splinter protruding like a dagger from between his ribs, called out '*Shinspu-sama* [Father], save me.' Some of the sights were sickening beyond words; the instinct was to look away in disgust. Two tiny holes peeked out of a masked piece of cartilage. There was no nose; it was as if it had been smudged by a heavy thumb. The woman's mouth was a lipless opening, a thin tear in an angry red face, like a squashed tomato.

At eight o'clock one of the workmen of the Novitiate arrived carrying a sack on his head.

'Father, I came upon this sack filled with little bottles that look like medicine.'

They were. They were phials of boric acid. This providential discovery of thirty pounds of antiseptic was to save many lives and lessen the pain of countless others. A solution of the antiseptic would be placed on the improvised bandages which were then placed on the wounds. The antiseptic solution would keep the lesions moist all day and in contact with the air. In this way the wounds were kept clean and the pain lessened. The discharge from the wounds would adhere to the dressing; by changing it four or five times a day asepsis was assured. In a few days' time a scar would begin to form which would slowly but surely bring about total healing.

The most common wounds were contusions caused by falling buildings and masonry. These included fractures and cuts produced by jagged pieces of tile and glass from falling roofs. Sometimes the fragments had penetrated the body without tearing the muscles. These were the comparatively lucky ones. But in most cases the skin and muscles had been torn. Dirt and sawdust were encrusted in these open wounds. These raw wounds had to be cleansed – but without anaesthetic, for no chloroform nor ether nor morphine was available to assuage the excruciating pain.

Just as horrific was the suffering caused by burns. When asked how they were burned the people would answer often that they had been trapped under a collapsed smouldering building and as they tried to extricate themselves from under it they were burned in the process. But there was another kind of burn which Father Arrupe could not account for. The victim would always state that he was not burnt at all.

'Then what happened to you?' the doctor-turned-priest would ask.

'I just saw a bright flash of light and then heard a gigantic explosion. But nothing happened to me. Then, in half an hour or so, small superficial blisters formed on my skin and in four or five hours huge burnt areas appeared on my body which soon became infected. But there was no fire.'

This baffled the doctor. Today we know the burns were due to infra-red radiation from the blast of the bomb. This radiation not only attacks the tissues and produces destruction of the epidermis and the endodermis but also damages the muscular tissue. The infections of these burns caused the death of many victims.

To cleanse the wounds it was necessary to puncture and open the blisters. As a blister was pierced drops of water would spill out. Sometimes the blisters were large, extending over half the body, and when these enormous blisters were punctured pails full of water would discharge. The suffering was frightful and the pain excruciating, causing the patients to writhe like snakes. But they never complained: they would suffer in silence, displaying tremendous self-control.

For several days funeral processions passed the House from morning until night, taking the dead to a small valley nearby where they were cremated. Until late at night the valley would be lit by funeral pyres. One day Father Luhmer and Father Laures were called to a house nearby. The frightful smell long before they reached it told them the occupant of the house had already died. They brought the bloated body to the valley and carried out the incineration themselves.

For days and weeks and months Father Arrupe and his priests-turned-medical-orderlies were kept busy tending the sick and wounded. This was a task they performed day and night, non-stop, catching snippets of sleep whenever they could. There was no one else to do the jobs of cleaning, wiping, daubing, winding, cleaning, wiping, daubing, winding.

Of the 260 doctors in the city before the explosion, 200 had perished. Of the sixty that remained many were wounded. Father Arrupe himself had found the Director of the Red Cross Hospital buried under the ruins of his house and had rescued him. He had six bone fractures and so was in no state to help anyone. Of the 1780 nurses, 1654 were dead or too badly injured to work. Most of the wounded fell into the hands of well-meaning but untrained or half-trained nurses. Sometimes it would have been better if they had not. It was a common sight to see interminable rows of 100 or 150 persons lying patiently in the streets while a 'nurse' walked up and down with a *fude* – a paint brush – with which she painted the wounds with some mercurochrome she carried in a can. Mercurochrome seemed the only medicine available. The mercury caused the destruction of body tissues.

If the 'technical' cures of the nurses were more harmful than good the home-made, 'domestic' cures were infinitely worse. The Japanese had a notion that the best cure for burns was the pulp of a turnip, which is plentiful in Hiroshima. Huge quantities of pulp were applied to the burns and wounds. The initial effect was refreshing. But after half an hour, with the hot August sun and the pus that was oozing from the wounds, a crust formed that caused unbearable pain. The family then tried to remedy this by applying a puree of potatoes which made the crust larger and though it began to look like a scar, there was obviously something soft remaining underneath. To absorb this they shook powder on the wound, sealing it with dust or ashes of vegetables. Finally, when the pain worsened they would try to relieve it by pouring on an oil, such as fish oil. The result would be the formation of a very hard black and shiny crust, like newly shone shoes. Father Arrupe and his assistants went from house to house telling people that these home-made cures spelt certain death and teaching them a simple healing process.

Father Arrupe recorded later his experiences of these horrendous days.

Among all the cases we treated, perhaps those that caused the most suffering were the children. At the time of the atomic bomb most of the children were in their respective schools. For that reason, during the explosion thousands of children were separated from their parents; many were wounded and cast into the streets without being able to fend for themselves. We brought all we could to Nagatsuka and began treating them immediately so as to prevent infection and fever.

We had absolutely no anaesthetics and some of the children were horribly wounded. One had a cut from ear to ear as a result of a beam that fell on his head. The edge of the wound was one and a half centimetres wide; the injured region of the scalp was filled with clay and pieces of glass. The screams of the poor child during his treatment so upset the entire house that we had no choice but to tie him into a cart with sheets and take him to the top of a hillock near the house. That spot was converted into an amphitheatre where we could work, and the child could scream all he wanted without making everyone else a nervous wreck.

Our hearts were torn apart during these treatments, but greater was the consolation at being able to restore the children to their parents. Through the Japanese police, who were well organized, we were able to contact all the families whose children we had in the house.

Memorable are those scenes of reunion with children that were thought dead in the explosion, and now were found alive and well, or at least in the process of healing. Those mothers and fathers, overcome with joy, did not know how to express their gratitude, throwing themselves at our feet.

Until the day after the explosion, we did not know that we were dealing with the first atomic bomb to explode in our world. At first, without electricity or radio, we were cut off from the rest of the world. The following day cars and trains began arriving from Tokyo and Osaka with help for Hiroshima.....

The knowledge that it was the atomic bomb that had exploded was no help to us at all from the medical standpoint, as no one in the world knew its full effects on the human organism. We were, in effect, the first guinea pigs in such experimentation.*

---

* Arrupe, Pedro, SJ, 'Surviving the Atom Bomb', in *Recollections and Reflections of Pedro Arrupe, SJ*, Michael Glazier, Wilmington, Delaware, 1986, p34f.

They were warned not to enter the city, because there was a gas in the air 'that kills for seventy years'. At such times, Arrupe reflected, when one knows that in the city there are 50 000 bodies which, unless they are cremated, will cause a terrible plague, and also some 120 000 wounded to care for, a priest cannot preserve his own life. When one is told that in the city there is a gas that kills, one must be very determined to ignore that fact and go in.

The priests from the Novitiate went into Hiroshima to find bodies and cremate them. They sifted the ruins of houses, to find whole families crushed beneath; they prevailed upon passers-by to raise pyramids of fifty or sixty bodies at a time and pour fuel on them to set them afire. With the August sun and the humid heat, it was soon easy to know where the bodies lay, using only the sense of smell. In this way the bodies dug out from the ruins or abandoned on the streets gradually disappeared.

For the first few hours after the catastrophe in Hiroshima no one in Tokyo knew what had happened. The first news was a telegram from the senior civil official of the Chugoku district that Hiroshima had been attacked by a 'small number of aircraft' which had used a 'wholly new type of bomb'. At dawn on 7 August General Kawabe, the Deputy Chief of General Staff, received a further report that was totally incomprehensible to him: 'The whole city of Hiroshima was destroyed instantly by a single bomb.'

Kawabe remembered that he had once been told of the possibility of an atom bomb. Without delay he sent for Professor Yoshio Nishina, Japan's leading atom scientist, who had studied under Niels Bohr in the 1920s.

'Could you build an atom bomb in six months?' he asked the small Japanese professor. Nishina had heard the American broadcast that an atom bomb had been dropped on Hiroshima, but he assumed that was just part of the propaganda war.

The General went on: 'In favourable circumstances we might be able to hold out that long.'

Nishina replied truthfully: 'Under present circumstances even six years would not be long enough. In any case we have no uranium.'

The next day (8 August) Nishina was put on an aircraft to find out the truth about Hiroshima. When his aircraft came within sight of the huge, smoking, pile of ruins that had once been a flourishing city, his fears were confirmed. Only a super weapon could have wreaked such devastation. All the grass round the airport was red, as if it had been toasted. On his arrival, the military officer in charge of Kamine airfield ran up to meet them. One half of his face was badly burned. It looked as if some foul disease that rotted flesh was trying to bore its way out from inside. The other half of his face was intact. Pointing to his burns (with fingers curled and webbed like talons clutching prey) he reported: 'Everything that was exposed was burned.'

Nishina began making his measurements. The tireless little man explored the city in all directions. By observing the side on which the telephone poles of *Cryptomeria japonica* all around the heart of the city had been charred he worked out that the centre of the blast had been a few yards south-east of the pile of ruins that had once been the Shima Hospital, and about 150 yards south of the *torii* gateway of Gokoku Shrine, next to the parade ground. He measured the extent to which windows had been shattered by the blast. The fact that the roof tiles of houses within a radius of some 650 yards of the point of explosion had melted to a thickness of 0.004 inches enabled him to compute the enormous temperatures which had developed. Mica (which has a melting point of 900°C) had fused on the granite of gravestones 400 yards from the centre. He estimated the bomb's heat at the centre must have been 600°C on the ground. From the shadows of human beings and objects, retained in the wood of some of the walls – the dazzling light had bleached and scorched everything around them – he was able to calculate the height at which the bomb exploded. He even dug up the ground 'on the spot right under the point of explosion' to calculate its radioactivity.*

He visited the anti-aircraft station on the island of Mukai Shima to get a description of the attack from the gunners. They told him: 'There were really only two B-29s. We can't believe they destroyed the whole city.'

Some days after the atomic bombing the Secretary of the University called on Father Arrupe and the other priests at Nagatsuka. He said the Japanese had invented a type of bomb, far more devastating than that used by the Americans, and were about to drop it on San Francisco. It is doubtful that he himself believed his story. He probably wanted to impress on the foreigners that the Japanese also could make such discoveries.

However, there was another atom bomb – but not on San Francisco.

---

* Four months later, in December 1945, Professor Nishina's whole body developed blotches which he believed to be a delayed result of the examination he had carried out of the radiation still in the debris.

Chapter Nine

Brother against Brother

Russia enters the war against Japan

On the morning of 8 August, Father Cieslik went into Hiroshima to look for Mr Fukai, the Japanese secretary of the diocese, who had been carried against his will out of the flaming city on Father Kleinsorge's back and then had run back into the inferno. Father Cieslik started hunting in the neighbourhood of Sakai Bridge, where the Jesuits had last seen Mr Fukai; he went to the East Parade Ground, the evacuation area to which the secretary might have gone, and looked for him among the wounded and dead there; he went to the prefectural police and made inquiries. He could not find any trace of the man.

Back at the Novitiate that evening, the theology student, who had shared a room with Mr Fukai at the Mission House, told the priests that the secretary had remarked to him, during an air-raid alarm one day not long before the bombing, 'Japan is dying. If there is a real air-raid here in Hiroshima, I want to die with our country.' The priests concluded that Mr Fukai had run back to immolate himself in the flames. They never saw him again.

When he got back to the Novitiate at Nagatsuka, Father Cieslik learned that Russia had declared war on Japan that day. Up to this time Russia had been 'neutral' against Japan. As long ago as February 1945 Japan, realizing any victory in the war was ebbing away, begged Russia, as a neutral, to act as an intermediary in arranging peace between Japan and the Western Allies. But nothing developed. Russia wanted to be in on the spoils of war. At the Yalta Conference in February Stalin had agreed to join the war against Japan provided he got the Kurile Islands, the whole of the island of Sakhalin and a controlling position in Manchuria. He stated that his reinforced armies in the Far East would be deployed by 8 August to attack the Japanese front in Manchuria.

Russia had waited until Japan was weak enough to be attacked with impunity. The next day Russian divisions, troops, tanks, flame-throwers, rolled into Manchuria and Sakhalin. Japan had always coveted Manchuria's rich mineral resources. In 1931 Japan's Imperial Kwantung Army invaded the country, including Sakhalin, separated from the eastern coast of Russia by the Tatarsk Sea, with the aim of making Manchuria a satellite state of Japan. Formerly Sakhalin had been used by Imperial Russia as a penal settlement. Anton Chekov, in his novel *Ostrov Sakhalin*, has described the appalling conditions under which the prisoners lived in the forests and tundra of the north and the dense deciduous growth of the south. During 1937 there were border skirmishes with Russia, who also had eyes on the rich minerals of Manchuria. There was further tension between Japan and Russia because Japan went to war with China in 1937 and Russia supported Mao Tse-Tung's communists in the fight against Japan. Tokyo responded by joining Hitler's Anti-Comintern Pact. Just as Hitler aimed to establish a 'new order' in Europe, Japan aimed to do likewise in the Far East. In April 1941 Japan signed a neutrality pact with Russia. But it still maintained fifteen divisions in Manchuria to oppose any Russian invasion.

Among those fifteen Japanese divisions was a young Jesuit novice, Mr Takeo Okurie, who had studied at the Novitiate until he was called up for military service. After graduating from the Jesuit Sophia University in Tokyo in 1941, he had decided to become a Jesuit. He did his training under Father Arrupe, who had just been appointed Master of Novices.

Until now Takeo's military service had been a more or less peaceable existence – as peaceable as things can be in a war. But now they were on full alert. At any moment the Russian onslaught would begin. And it would be a huge onslaught. It was some months since the war in Europe had ended. A fresh, heavily reinforced Russian army was poised to attack an army whose morale was low after loss after loss in the Pacific theatre, whose rations had been cut and cut as the mainland became more and more cut off. But their spirits were high. The Japanese would fight to the death. There would be no surrender. Japanese officers cleaned their *wakizashis* – short-bladed knives – with which they would commit *harakiri* rather than surrender. Takeo Okurie didn't clean his. In fact, he didn't possess one since taking one's own life was against his Christian morals.

His colonel was a true Samurai, courageous, just, benevolent, polite, honest, loyal and compassionate. He would never surrender. He would perish for the imperial honour, however doomed the cause. Three stars glittering on his red and gold tabs on his collar and, clutching his sword, he went from group to group, giving encouragement and exhortation.

'*Tenno-heika, Banzai, Banzai, Banzai,*' he shouted, the *Banzai* call when about to die for the Emperor.He reminded his fellow officers of what Kendo, a court official turned Buddhist monk, had written around AD 1330 in a Book of Essays called *Tsurezure-gusa*: 'Only if a man accepts death calmly when his sword is broken and his arrows spent, to the end refusing surrender, does he prove he is a hero.'

Takeo recalled from his studies the last rule of St Ignatius: 'As in the whole of life, so also in death, everyone in the Society must take care that God our Lord be glorified in him and that those around be edified by the example of his fortitude.'

Takeo sat with his unit in their well-prepared foxholes. They waited – and waited. The sun had long since set; the twilight too had yielded to the night. By now his eyes were getting heavy with sleep. But sleep he must not. He pulled out his Rosary. Some of his colleagues used to tease him about his practices, such as letting the beads slip through his fingers, that this 'smelt of butter' – their reference to Western ideas. Tonight they had other things on their minds.

Appropriately enough he began the Sorrowful Mysteries. The Agony in the Garden: 'Yes', he thought, that must have been much, much worse than he was suffering now. The Scourging at the Pillar; The Crowning with Thorns; Jesus Carries His Cross. His tired mind began to wander. It was hard to concentrate. He began to think of his early care-free, happy days. He thought of his short but happy life; of his days at the Novitiate; he wondered what his fellow-novices were doing now. Were they all in the army like he was? He remembered his arrival at the Novitiate – the walk from the city centre to Nagatsuka, about a mile and a half from Hiroshima, half-way up the sides of a broad valley which stretched from the city centre at sea level into the moutainous hinterland.

The *haru-gasumi*, the faint blue haze that shrouds the mountains in spring, was barely visible. The morning sun glinted off a river as it coursed its way down to the sea. It was *Horta-age*, the Kite Flying Festival. He smiled as he looked up at hundreds of multi-coloured kites soaring, diving, and swerving as their puppeteers strove to cut each other's string. A papier-maché case held all his possessions. He had been told to bring only the barest of essentials. He passed the quaint thatch-roofed houses of the farmers that had been handed down from generation to generation. They were thatched with *susuki*, miscanthus reed, a frailer Japanese variety of pampas grass. The thick thatch made the houses cooler in summer and warmer in winter, and also blended in beautifully with the rice fields. Women were singing as they weeded in the rice paddies. Dragonflies – hundreds of them – darted ceaselessly over the burning waters. One woman called out to him to help her pull off a leech on her arm. He smiled and carried on. Past the fields of carrots and radishes and potatoes. Soon he was in the cooler, fresh air of the hills that ringed the city. Majestic Himalayan cypresses gazed down on him. The south-east wind off the Seto Sea set the pines to creaking. Here and there groves of scrub bamboo and of hemp-palm and camphor laurels and chestnuts had infiltrated among the older trees gossiping in the cool breeze. The wild flowers – he had never seen such a variety.

The sun was now high in the pine trees. He sat down and rested in the grounds of the Night of the Lotus Temple, of the Jodo Shinsu sect of Buddhism. A fig tree, a tangantangan tree and a katsura tree kept him company. He listened to the birds as they trilled against the monotone pizzicato of the summer cicadas. It was the first time he had ever heard the *uguisu*, the bush warbler or Japanese nightingale. Some women were returning home carrying firewood on their backs which they had collected in the woods.

He arrived at what looked like another Buddhist temple. But this was not a temple: it was the Novitiate. He approached the wooden building, complete with pointed roofs and a pagoda of three floors with red roofs and a bell tower topped with a cross. The booms of the bell rang out across the countryside, ringing the *Angelus*; it must be mid-day. He was taken aback by the garden. He had never seen such a beautiful display of colour – Chinese bellflowers, dahlias, chrysanthemums, azaleas, persimmons, blood red oleander and cannas, everywhere in magnificent bloom. The cherry blossoms and maples still had their colours. Little did he know it then, but he would be spending many, many hours in those gardens and vegetable fields. Practical work in the garden and fields has always been an important part of Jesuit training. It gave one time to appreciate nature, the seasons, the dawn, the evening sky, life in all its wondrous beauty; time to search out the hidden beauty that is everywhere and to discover the glorious things around us. Then each day becomes a *haiku* poem. It was said that some people make a living writing *haiku* poetry; we should make our living like *haiku* poetry.

He walked up to the entrance and rang the bell. He was greeted by a man in black trousers and open-neck white shirt. He assumed he was one of the priests – but he wasn't. He was Brother Gropper, who had started building the Novitiate in 1937, finishing it two years later.

Takeo was shown to his bare room; he was introduced to his fellow-novices. He remembered how at first the rather austere-looking Novice Master had filled him with some trepidation. Father Arrupe was a man who drove himself hard, getting by with just five hours sleep a day. He would be up early every day for his prayers. But he was anything than a grim-faced ascetic. He bubbled over with high spirits and laughed a lot, especially at jokes against himself. He showed no airs or graces. He was totally devoid of affectation, totally unassuming. There was not a dewdrop's weight of pomp or condescension in him. The lack of self-importance and pride that he hoped to instil in his novices was exemplified in his own life. The novices admired and loved him.

Why did he want to be a Jesuit? Takeo remembered being asked. Why indeed? And he remembered his answer: it was the Japanese martyrs – men like Paul Miki. The atheistic form of existentialism that was then popular among Japanese university studies left him cold. But heroes like Miki inspired him. Saint Francis Xavier had planted Christianity in Japan when he arrived in 1549. By 1587 there were over 200 000 Christians in Japan. In that year the Regent Hideyoshi ordered all missionaries out of his dominions. Some left, but many stayed on in disguise.

In 1596 the Regent was roused to fury by the boast of the captain of a Spanish ship that the true purpose of the missionaries was to facilitate the conquest of Japan by the Portuguese or Spaniards. Enraged, the Regent ordered the execution of all missionaries. In 1597 three Jesuits and one Franciscan were crucified on Nishizaka Hill near Nagasaki. One of the Jesuits was thirty-three year old Paul Miki, a high-born Japanese, the son of a general in Baron Takayama's army. The missionaries first had part of their left ears cut off and were then led through various towns and villages, their cheeks covered with blood, as a warning to the people. At the place of execution they were fastened to crosses by cords and straw ropes, iron chains about their arms and legs and with iron collars round their necks. The crosses were then raised into the air, the foot of each cross falling into a hole in the ground specially dug for it. The crosses were planted in a row, about four feet apart. Two samurai executioners, unsheathed bamboo spears ready to hand, stood by each cross. A signal was given and the executioners thrust their lances under the rib cages and through the hearts of their victims. The blood and garments of the martyrs were later collected by 'underground' Christians. Paul Miki and his companions were canonized as saints in 1862.

In addition to the priests, a total of twenty-six other Christians were martyred that day. The twenty-six neatly drawn-up crosses ran from the brow of Nishizaka Hill, near the present railway station of Nagasaki, down towards the harbour so that everyone could see the spectacle. The Togakawa Shoguns saw Christianity as an alien thing that must be exterminated. In the seventeenth century tens of thousands of Japanese Christians were put to death. The Togakawa dictators and later the Militarists branded Japanese Christians as traitors to the *kokutai*, the unique Japanese national polity. That was why class-conscious Japanese could never be Christians. And that was why many of his fellow-recruits in the army mocked Takeo Okurie.

Waiting for the Russian assault, Takeo prayed that if he had to die he would, at the moment of death, – 'the moment of ultimate honesty', as Pascal called it – die as bravely. He remembered with laughter the fun the children used to poke at him as he tramped round Hiroshima collecting horse manure. In order to produce men who would be 'dead to the world', humble and without pride, Father Arrupe used to send the novices through the city picking up horse manure for the garden. The children would run up to him singing:

'Here comes the horse-dung man. Hold your noses if your can!'

He would laugh and chase after them. Any delusions of pride and self importance that he still might have harboured soon evaporated. He would quite happily exchange his position now for that of horse-dung collector in Hiroshima. Of course, he had no idea what had happened to the city just two days earlier. To avoid panic the Japanese public were told nothing about the Hiroshima holocaust. Even the Prime Minister himself at first refused to believe the reports that a single bomb had caused so much destruction. The rest of Japan did not know about the atomic bombing of the city until after the war.

Takeo thought of the very many happy hours he spent in the garden and the fields so as to gain practical experimental wisdom. For equilibrium and mental peace he would learn *shodo* (beautiful Japanese hand-writing).

The prospect of any equilibrium and mental peace was suddenly shattered by the horrendous din of a massive artillery bombardment. The acrid smell of cordite fouled the air. This was the prelude to a dawn offensive by hundreds of Red Army tanks and aircraft that swamped their positions like a tidal wave. The Japanese fought with their customary tenacity. But lacking heavy tanks and air support, their positions were soon over-run. Their dead lay everywhere. Among the dead lay Takeo Okurie. It was 10 August 1945.

✢✣

Takeo was not the only Jesuit who had been involved in active service in this war. There was also Josef Kotetsa Matsumora, born on 13 January 1913, in Amami O Shima, the northernmost of the Ryukyu Islands, south of the large Japanese island of Kyushu. At an early age he expressed a wish to become a priest. He went to the Minor Seminary in Nagasaki to begin his studies for the priesthood. He then went on to the Regional Seminary in Tokyo.

He decided he would like to become a Jesuit, like his heroes the Jesuits Saint Francis Xavier and the Japanese martyr Paul Miki. On 12

April 1939 he arrived at the Novitiate at Nagatsuka to begin his training for the Society of Jesus.

But already the clouds of war were in the air. The morality of war worried the young novice. How could a Christian accept war with all its killing and suffering? The teaching of the Church on the subject had been laid down by Saint Augustine in the fourth century – one could fight a just war. The Japanese military propaganda machine had skilfully argued the justness of their war. Japan had a sacred responsibility to occupy the political vacuum in Manchuria and stop the spread of inhuman Bolshevism. Japan also had a duty to liberate Asia from western colonists like Britain and usher in the Asia Co- prosperity era. Britain, not America, was the real enemy. They wanted to throw this Western intruder out of Asia and return Asia to the Asians. But one obstacle stood in the way: the American fleet. If it could be eliminated, in one sudden attack, while it slept peacefully at Pearl Harbour, the 'effete' Americans could be neutralized, and Asia liberated.

After only four months at the Novitiate Matsumora was called up on the Feast of the Assumption, 15 August, 1939. He was told to report to the army in his home province which was Kagoshima. Kagoshima was, oddly enough, the first place where Francis Xavier had landed in Japan in 1549. One day in 1940, his army training completed, Matsumora set sail, with thousands of other young Japanese, in a convoy of twenty ships taking them ... he knew not where. Over the next few months he struggled against heat and rain and malaria and dysentery and jungle rot in the Solomon Islands – not to mention the US marines who were later to land on the same islands and engage the Japanese in the bloodiest battles, often hand to hand, in the whole war.

The ethics and morality of war remained a matter of great concern to the young man. At the Novitiate he had had long discussions on the subject of war. He couldn't reconcile himself to the thought of people killing people, no matter how just the cause for war. He often used to wonder what he would do if he ever encountered an 'enemy' Jesuit. After all there were 243 Jesuits serving as Chaplains in the United States armed forces.

❦

One of them was Carl Hausmann, a forty-three year old American Army Chaplain serving in the Philippines. Hausmann was taken prisoner-of-war in December 1941. He spent the next three years slaving in a penal colony in terrible conditions: hunger, thirst, long days in the boiling sun, dysentery, and worst of all, constant harassment and humiliation, constant bowing to guards who were just plain thugs. Hundreds of men slept together, sweating, shivering with malaria, turning yellow with hepatitis. Hausmann conducted more funerals than he had in all his life.

By 1944 the war was going badly for Japan in the Philippines. General Yamashita ordered all prisoners of war to be taken to Japan. In mid-December 1944, the *Oroyku Maru* set sail for Japan with 1600 prisoners on board, including Father Carl Hausmann. But the ship didn't get very far. For a night and a day American aircraft bombed and strafed the ship.

The prisoners were all battened down in the hatches below, listening to the bombs and shells bursting on the deck above. Finally the cargo vessel was driven aground on the shore of Subic Bay, west of the peninsula of Bataan. The *Oroyku Maru* was a sitting duck. She suffered three direct hits. The prisoners below deck made a desperate rush for the ladders. The Japanese guards forced them back, firing point blank into their faces. Then the ship caught fire from stem to stern. The Japanese crew and guards jumped ship. The prisoners, too, including Hausmann, leaped into the shark-infested waters of the Pacific and swam for the shore. Many drowned. Those who made it to the shore were met by a battalion of Japanese infantry. And many who survived the waves and the sharks didn't survive the bullets. The Japanese machine-gunned many as they scrambled onto the beach; others they took prisoner. Hausmann and two others floated ashore and were captured.

They were bundled into another freighter bound for Japan. Again the B-29s caught up with it off the coast of Formosa (now Taiwan) in the East China Sea. The forward hold suffered a direct hit. The Japanese crew and guards looked down into the welter of skeletons and sealed the hold completely. The living were pinned under the dead in the airless darkness and the stench. Daylight brought heat and suffocation. Forty-eight hours later the ship limped into harbour. Of the 500 men sealed alive in the hold only seven were still breathing. The dead were hauled up in a wire loading net and dumped into a waiting barge.

The rest of the voyage was even more ghastly and harrowing. All they got for food was a half-cup of rice every three days. Every morning those of the survivors who had succumbed were hauled up and tossed overboard. Among the remaining few personal grudges surfaced; men would be found with their throats or stomachs slit open. A man slashed his neighbour to death – in order to drink his blood. Thirst and hunger, stench and flies by the thousand, festering wounds and overflowing latrine cans, despair and madness. In the

end Carl Hausmann too succumbed. In this corner of hell he made his
last confession and died.

The guards stripped off what few rags he was wearing and hurled
them to the living. The boatswain tied a rope around his knees and
neck and the body, gaunt and naked, was lifted slowly through the
hatch, to be thrown overboard or used as fuel.

That was one 'enemy' Jesuit Josef Matsumora would not
encounter.

In the same stretch of waters off the coast of Formosa where Father
Hausmann, as an American prisoner on a Japanese ship, had been
bombed by American B-29s, a fellow American Jesuit, Father Joseph
O'Callahan, on an American aircraft carrier, the USS *Franklin*, was
being bombed by a Japanese *kamikaze* pilot.

On Saturday 17 March the forty-year-old Jesuit said Mass for 1200
men on the fo'c'sle of the carrier. This wasn't because it was Sunday
or a holy day or even because it happened to be St Patrick's Day. It
was the last Mass before combat. One third of the ship's complement
crowded on to the fo'c'sle to witness the Transfiguration and
Immolation. Before tomorrow was done, most of those on the fo'c'sle
would have crossed to eternity.

The next morning a tremendous explosion shot O'Callahan out
of his bunk. Then another, even more shattering and deafening.
A fanatical *kamikaze* pilot, probably under the influence of hiropon,
a drug that induced a sensation of great well-being and energy, came
in a screaming dive out of the overcast sky, and crashed his
Mitsubishi aircraft through the flight deck. There were hundreds of
planes on the flight and hangar decks, their tanks filled with many
gallons of high octane gas; both planes and ship were also laden with
thousands of 1000-lb and 2000-lb bombs, each capable of blowing up
a whole battleship. Soon the whole deck was 'just one solid mass of fire'.

In May 1945 a historic award presentation ceremony took place on
board the USS *Franklin* in Brooklyn Navy Yard. A total of 393 awards
for gallantry were presented to the crew of one ship for heroism on
one day's combat. Father O'Callaghan's mother listened as the
citations were read. Her son was not mentioned. Perhaps chaplains
were not considered for such awards. But later Captain Les Gehres,
commander of the USS *Franklin*, came up to her.

'I am not a religious man,' he said, 'But during the height of
combat, while I watched your son, I said aloud then, as I say to you
now, "If Faith can do that for a man, there must be something in it".'

When Mrs O'Callaghan arrived home there was a letter waiting for her. It was an invitation to attend a ceremony at the White House at which the President would present her son with the Congressional Medal of Honour, America's highest honour for bravery. He was the first chaplain ever to be given this award. It was given for:

> conspicuous gallantry and intrepidity at the risk of his life above and beyond the call of duty...when [the USS *Franklin*] was fiercely attacked by enemy Japanese aircraft on 19 March 1945...With the ship rocked by incessant explosions, with debris and fragments raining down and fires raging in ever increasing fury, he ministered to the wounded and dying, comforting and encouraging men of all faiths.... Serving with courage, fortitude and deep spiritual strength, Lieutenant Commander O'Callaghan inspired the gallant officers and men of the Franklin to fight heroically and with profound faith in the face of almost certain death and return their stricken ship to port.

On the very day when Father O'Callahan was risking his life on the USS *Franklin*, Josef Matsumora was in Bougainville, awaiting the next great push by the advancing American forces.

In March 1942 the Japanese had occupied Bougainville during their drive down through the South Pacific islands on their way to Australia. By July 1942 they had reached as far south as the Solomon Islands and northern Papua and New Guinea. The Marist missionaries on the island of Bougainville were all then taken prisoner and interned.

One day two Japanese soldiers had appeared in the courtyard of the Mission. If they had not come to arrest and take away prisoners, they would be demanding food and produce from the garden and agricultural plots the locals tended. They were in green uniform, wearing peaked caps. They carried rifles.

Father Adam went out to meet them. One of the soldiers was a young man, thin and hungry-looking as everyone on Bougainville was those days. His mouth opened in a wide smile. Father Adam was taken aback. He had become used to the curt bullying orders of the soldiers. He was even more surprised when the soldier clicked his heels and bowed low. His green shirt was soaked with sweat as were his trousers bound by puttees at the ankles. A cape hung from the back of his cap to keep the sun off his neck.

The soldier began to talk. He soon realized Father Adam didn't understand a word he was saying. Father Adam ventured into Latin. The soldier smiled even wider. He also knew some Latin. By means of signs and some simple and familiar Church Latin phrases the soldier began to make himself understood.

The soldier's name was Matsumora. He was studying to become a Jesuit priest at the Novitiate in Hiroshima. His novice master was a Father Andreas Schiffer. He wanted a Bible and a rosary. Father Adam gave these to him. The soldier bowed, clicked his heels and left with his colleague.

Matsumora visited the Mission quite often after that, carrying on a stilted conversation through the medium of Church Latin. He always made a point of visiting the Blessed Sacrament. On occasion the priests were allowed to visit and minister to nearby villages providing they were accompanied by Japanese guards. Matsumora volunteered to be one such guard and enjoyed accompanying the priests into the jungle since this also enabled him to hear Mass and go to Communion.

It was the Feast of the Annunciation of the Lord, 25 March 1945. Matsumora had attended the Mass said by Father Muller that morning. He was in the plantation while Father Muller supervised the agricultural work. Three Japanese soldiers, their rifles cocked, kept guard. Little did they know that six pairs of eyes were watching them from the silent, sweating jungle adjoining the garden. Sergeant-Major Paias Jaintong, of the Native Militia, armed by the Australian forces, was dressed only in a *lap-lap* round his waist. His ebony-black body gleamed with perspiration. He turned to catch the eyes of his patrol. A tusk of a wild pig went through the septum of his broad nostrils. If he was ever cornered by the Japanese all he had to do was hide his automatic weapons in the bush and he would instantaneously become just another plain, harmless, local, Bougainville 'savage'. He adjusted the bandoleer he carried round his burly shoulders.

Father Muller was tired. He sat on a fallen tree for a rest. Matsumora joined him. A catechist sat beside Father Muller on the other side. Suddenly there was a commotion, followed by rifle shots. The catechist grabbed Father Muller and told him not to move. They were surrounded by Sergeant-Major Jaintong's black soldiers of the local militia. In no time at all the Japanese soldiers had been killed. Matsumora along with them. At last his war was over. His new life began.

That afternoon the body of the Jesuit seminarian was laid to rest in the missionaries' cemetery in Kieta. That evening Father Muller wrote to the Jesuit Novitiate in Hiroshima, expressing gratitude at how much their seminarian had helped them in their missionary activities and how well he had died.

Chapter Ten

The 'Fat Man' and surrender

9–15 August 1945

President Harry Truman heard the news of Hiroshima at lunchtime on 6 August while returning from the Potsdam Conference on the cruiser *Augusta*. He broadcast another – still more urgent – plea to Japan to surrender.

> It is an atomic bomb. It is a harnessing of the basic power of the universe. The force from which the sun draws its power has been loosed against those who brought war to the Far East ... It was to spare the Japanese people from utter destruction that the ultimatum of the 27th was issued from Potsdam. Their leaders promptly rejected that ultimatum. If they do not now accept our terms, they may expect a rain of ruin from the air the like of which has never been seen on this earth.

Japan had a small atomic research programme. In 1935 the Japanese physicist Hikedi Yukawa predicted the discovery of the meson, a nuclear particle required theoretically to bind the protons of an atomic nucleus. (In 1949 Yukawa was the first Japanese to win the Nobel Prize for this research.) There was also the nuclear physicist Professor Sagari, who had worked with Luis Alvarez at the University of California. The good humoured Japanese physicist Shinoza had developed a cloud chamber that automatically photographed the path of atoms. Unfortunately the Japanese government had little knowledge of this rarefied research going on in the groves of academe. The majority of people had not the slightest idea of what the word 'atomic' meant. They took Truman's dramatic announcement as just another propaganda ploy.

Again, leaflets were dropped, advising the population to evacuate the target areas of Kokura and Nagasaki. Some leaflets were even put to rhyme: 'In April Nagasaki was all flowers; in August it will be flame showers.'

People were forbidden to read the leaflets. Those who did regarded them as so much *agitprop* and dismissed them.

Group Captain Cheshire was excited as he ate the customary breakfast before take off. Waiting on the runway at the Tinian air field was *Bock's Car*, a Superfortress (named after its regular pilot Captain Bock) that was about to deliver a second atom bomb on Japan. Cheshire and Robert Penney would not be on *Bock's Car*, but they would be accompanying it in another B-29 as part of the observer crew. He had been disappointed to miss accompanying the *Enola Gay* when it dropped the 'Thin Man' on Hiroshima. Tonight he would be helping to make history with the 'Fat Man'.

The Thin Man had been a uranium atom bomb. The Fat Man was of plutonium. This bomb was called the Fat Man, because it was much stubbier, though shorter, than the Hiroshima bomb. It was ten feet eight inches long and five feet in diameter. It was shaped, in fact, like a barrage balloon or zeppelin. Whereas the Thin Man's detonation over Hiroshima was not a foregone conclusion, since a bomb of that kind had never been tested, the success of the Fat Man was more assured since it was identical to the bomb tested less than a month earlier at Alamogordo, in New Mexico.

The Fat Man lay tucked up in the belly of *Bock's Car*. Tonight, however, the pilot was not Bock but Major Charles W. Sweeney, a happy-go-lucky pilot for one flying such an onerous mission. Perhaps it was as well he was happy-go-lucky.

The attack with the Fat Man had originally been planned for 20 August. Then the date was brought forward by nine days to 11 August. But a five-day spell of bad weather was forecast, beginning on 10 August. It was necessary to bring forward the date even more. Then on 8 August Russia declared war on Japan. There were some who argued that a second atomic attack on Japan was unnecessary. Once the extent of the devastation in Hiroshima reached the Japanese public they would sue for peace. But if Russia was at war with Japan, she could claim part of the spoils of victory. To deny her these, it was decided to bring forward the date of the attack to 9 August. Not only would that prevent the Soviets from claiming a real part in the victory over Japan, it might even warn the Russian giant of the future dangers of too ambitious and vociferous an appetite. Since the end of the War in Europe the activities of the Soviet government in the Eastern European countries, especially Poland, had made it abundantly clear that Stalin had no intention of complying with earlier agreements with the Western Allies, and was bent on bringing Eastern Europe into the Soviet bloc.

With hindsight we may argue whether the ultimate weapon, the atom bomb, should have been used. It certainly saved lives in the long run – no invasion was necessary. But then there were many, civilian and military, who advised Truman that a Japanese surrender could be got without an invasion. That was disputable. Even after

Hiroshima the military die hards who ruled Japan rejected surrender out of hand. Recent documents suggest that the decision to drop the bombs on Hiroshima and Nagasaki had little, if anything, to do with calculations and comparisons of likely casualties following an invasion, but everything to do with the diplomatic strategy for containing the Soviet Union in the post-war world.* Moreover – unbeknown to Truman and the few who were party to the atom bomb secret – at that very time, despite the most intensive security precautions ever mounted, agents had already passed on to the Soviets secrets of the tests in the Alamogordo.

The logistics and bombing plan were much the same as with the *Enola Gay*. *Bock's Car* would be preceded by a weather plane and accompanied by a B-29 carrying monitoring equipment and another B-29, a camera plane, with observers, which would include the British contingent of Cheshire and Penney.

Before take-off a senior naval officer reminded Major 'Chuck' Sweeney that the Fat Man had cost $25 million, and warned him to 'get our money's worth'. The navy man's estimate was low by many orders of magnitude – together with the Thin Man, Fat Man had actually cost over two billion. But Sweeney did not know that, and even $25 million swinging in his B-29's bomb bay must have seemed an astronomical sum to an officer who drew less than $400 pay a month.

The primary target was Kokura, on the northern tip of Kyushu, a huge army arsenal. From the start things began to happen that soon changed Sweeney's happy-go- lucky demeanour. His take-off before dawn, loaded as he was with the four-and-a-half-ton Fat Man, was quite a hair-raising affair. Then technical snags occurred in arming the bomb. The weather reports were bad and getting worse. By the time he was over Kukura, the city was completely hidden under cloud. He had strict orders to bomb only if his target was clearly visible. It was not visible at all. In addition smoke from factory chimneys further hid his aiming point. He made three passes over the city hoping the clouds and smoke would clear. They did not. And then he made a disconcerting discovery: he was fast running out of gasoline. Due to a faulty fuel pump he had 600 gallons of fuel that he couldn't use trapped in his bomb-bay tank. He had already been circling over the city for three-quarters of an hour. He couldn't waste any more time – or fuel. He could just make it back to base in Tinian. But he could not return to Tinian and attempt landing with the 'Fat Man' on board. If he crashed he would not only blow up himself and his crew and *Bock's Car*, but also most of Tinian.

---

* Gar Alperowitz, *Atomic Diplomacy*, Pluto Publishing Ltd, London, 1985.

His alternative target was Nagasaki. At least that was on the way back. The weather planes had reported that city under clouds. Sweeney swung his Superfortress south-west and headed for the much bigger city of Nagasaki, with a population of a quarter of a million. By the time he reached Nagasaki he had fuel only for one run. He decided to disobey his orders and begin his bomb run by radar. Just before 11 a.m. the B-29 was over Shimabara. A radio announcer on the ground saw the plane and excitedly broadcast a warning; people who heard him made for the shelters.

Just then Sweeney and his bombardier, Captain Kermit Beahan, got a lucky break. They saw Nagasaki right below them through a break in the clouds. Beahan recognized the Urakami River and the Matsuyama Sports Ground. They were over two miles north-west of the planned drop. But time had run out. Kermit pressed the pickle-switch, which released the Fat Man. It was exactly 11 a.m. The bomb fell out of the bomb bay and went plummeting down, gathering pace as it did so, on to the city of 200000 people, of whom more than 70000 would die, many without a trace. Another *deus ex machina* had been released on the world.

At 11.02 the plutonium bomb detonated at 1500 feet above the Urakami district of the city, where the factories, schools and residences were concentrated, but thirty-six blocks away from the intended point of explosion. Like Hiroshima, Nagasaki was a city of wooden structures.

The visual effects and the blast and radiation phenomena were much the same as occurred on the first test at Alamogordo and at Hiroshima. The velocity of the wind that rushed out from the epicentre was sixty times the speed of a major hurricane – 1.24 miles per second. This caused a vacuum at the epicentre and another cyclone rushed back in to take its place, sucking up acres of dust, dirt, debris and smoke.

A huge white cloud rose up. The cloud was white on the outside but fired by some hideous red energy within. Then came alternating flashes of red, yellow, purple. Gradually the cloud grew into a writhing mushroom shape, slowly flattening itself as if by magic and a black stain grew on its stem. When the cloud reached a great height it burst open and collapsed. Then came a roar of wind so strong it seemed as if another bomb had exploded nearby.

Cheshire, like everyone else on the plane was elated. The bomb had detonated; they had hit the target. But he was also shocked. He had never seen anything like this on his many air-raids over Germany. As he watched the swirling, angry clouds and smoke billow heavenwards, spewing their anger at whatever Powers there might be, he realized the casualties would have been staggering. He took some comfort from the thought that, huge as the casualties were, they were a trifle compared to what would happen if there was an invasion. As a military man he realized, too, that the hardened Japanese military would never surrender under conditions of normal warfare. Only some stupendous weapon never yet dreamed of would perhaps change their minds. Even after Hiroshima the die-hards had refused to surrender. Would they surrender now? Or would a third bomb be necessary? – except that there was no third bomb.

The detonation of the Fat Man bomb generated a fireball of destruction that carbonized 35 000 people instantly and flattened the centre of the city. Houses, buildings, trees – anything standing – were cut down as if by some enormous, invisible, bull-dozer. But the extent of the damage was contained because an eight-hundred-foot ridge of hills protected the militarily more important part of the city – the Nakashima district – where the prefectural, municipal and other governmental offices were located. Although the Fat Man was a much stronger bomb than the Thin Man, due to Beahan's hurried aim the damage in Nagasaki was only about a quarter as effective as in Hiroshima, the effective damage in the second city to be destroyed by an atom bomb being restricted to an area of about four square miles.

At 11 a.m. on 9 August 1945, just as the Fat Man was hurtling through the sky to wreak its horrendous havoc, the six members of the Japanese Supreme Council of War sat down to discuss the surrender demands of the Potsdam Conference in the light of what had happened at Hiroshima. The arguments between the militarists and the peace faction waxed to and fro between the protagonists of war and of peace. The Foreign Minister Togo, backed by the Prime Minister Suzuki and the Navy Minister Admiral Yonai argued that Japan had no choice but to accept the Potsdam terms of surrender. The other three members of the War Council were adamantly opposed to any surrender. These three were the War Minister General Anami, Army Chief General Umezu and Navy Chief Admiral Toyoda. War Minister Anami would not accept that the Imperial Army would ever surrender; they must fight to the end, to 'find life in death'. The Commanders of the Pacific islands recaptured by the Americans had ordered their men to fight to the very last drop of blood and had then almost all themselves committed ceremonial *hara-kiri*; how could the defenders of the home islands betray such an example? Japan could not be ringed by battleships and was over 90 per cent mountain. The Americans might land on the coastal plains but the Imperial Army and the adult population would fall back to the next mountains and to the next. The Americans would have to fight for years and lose millions of men – or change those 'unconditional surrender' terms with the blasphemous possibility of trying and executing the Emperor. Every Japanese would die a thousand deaths rather than allow that. The deadlock was hopeless and the meeting abandoned.

Some hours later the news of the bomb on Nagasaki was received. The Emperor summoned the Supreme War Council, all cabinet ministers and senior imperial officials to meet him at midnight in his air-raid shelter. The two factions were prepared to continue their arguments. Admiral Suzuki wearily suggested they should ask the Emperor to express his wishes. The Emperor did. Small, round-shouldered, near-sighted and very shy, the Emperor began. In a piping, almost expressionless, voice he denounced the futility of 'prolongation of the bloodshed and cruelty'. He agreed that the terms of Potsdam, calling for the disarming of the armed forces and the punishment of war leaders were 'unbearable'.

'Nevertheless,' he added, 'the time has come when we must bear the unbearable.'

Ministers began to sob; the Emperor wiped his cheeks with white-gloved hands. He would make an address to the nation at noon the next morning, 15 August 1945.

During the night an assassination attempt, led by Major Kari Hatamaka, a fanatical army staff officer, was made on the life of the Emperor, so that he could not broadcast a surrender. But the plot did not succeed. On the morning of 15 August 'announcement teams' of military policemen drove over the acres of ruin in Hiroshima and Nagaski and also through other cities and towns of Japan announcing:

Attention everyone! Attention. Today at 12 noon the Emperor in person will make an important announcement over the radio. All who are capable of moving should make their way to the railway station [or other such prominent location], where the Emperor's speech will be relayed over the loudspeaker system.

A few hundred persons, in rags, wounded, sick, leaning on sticks or crutches, gathered on the square in front of the flattened, burnt out, Yokogawa railway station in Hiroshima. At the Novitiate a loudspeaker had been installed in the garden so that the priests and others could hear the Emperor. Millions, in other parts of Japan, stood silent before their radio sets. Just before noon a Lieutenant called 'Attention!' and everyone in the NHK studio in Tokyo rose. The officer announced: 'This will be a broadcast of the gravest importance. Will all listeners please rise.'

Soldiers stood stiffly to attention, young civilians lowered their heads, the older knelt to the ground, their faces almost touching the dust, as a nervous, reedy, high-pitched monotone voice they had never heard before trembled, as if on the verge of tears. It was their Emperor and High Priest of Shinto speaking from the Chrysanthemum Throne. He began to deliver, in the accent of the court of Japan, the shocking news of defeat. Many were expecting Tenno, the Emperor, to announce final victory.

After pondering deeply the general trends of the world and the actual conditions obtaining in Our Empire today ... and since Russia had entered the war and since America had those terrible weapons of destruction ... and since I am responsible for the lives of 84 million subjects ... in order to avoid further bloodshed, perhaps even the total extinction of civilization ... prepare to endure the unendurable, to suffer the insufferable ... We have decided to effect a settlement of the present situation by resorting to an extraordinary measure ... We have ordered our Government to communicate with the Governments of the United States, Great Britain and the Soviet Union that our Empire accepts the provisions of the Potsdam Joint Declaration ...

The terms of the declaration had demanded unconditional surrender.

Tears of agonized disbelief were shed by both civilians and military in Japan and by the soldiers still guarding the defences of a crumbling empire. The news broadcasts throughout the war had never once reported a defeat or retreat. By 1942 the American Navy had cracked the Japanese Code. Tokyo's plans for the Battle of Midway were studied in advance by the US Navy. So, in June 1942, when a huge Japanese task force set off it steamed straight into the grey jaws of a steel trap set by Admiral Nimitz. The Japanese lost four big aircraft carriers and the best of their Fleet Air Arm. Never again was Japan able to wrest the naval initiative. But the Japanese public were never given any inkling of these reverses. The great defeats at Bougainville, in the Solomons and most recently at Okinawa were never mentioned. Most Japanese were steadfast in their belief that continued efforts and sacrifices would lead to ultimate victory. The sudden shock of defeat was too much to bear. A vast throng had gathered in front of the Imperial Palace in Tokyo. In the outpouring of national sorrow the crowd paid little attention to those zealous army officers who chose to commit *hara-kiri* rather than accept the share of their country's first military defeat in more than two and a half thousand years. The radio blared 'Kimi ga yo', the national anthem.

In a sense, the atom bombs gave Japan the perfect face-saving excuse for surrender. They could now pretend that an almost supernatural element had intervened to force them into defeat. For the Allies, too, there was reason to be pleased: the nightmare of an invasion of Japan was cancelled, saving perhaps half a million American and several million Japanese lives.

Of course, the surrender, while most welcome, had come too late for Carl Hausmann and Takeo Okurie and Josef Matsumora and millions of others on both sides. Since all-out war with China began in 1937 until the peace in August 1945, 2.5 million Japanese had died 1 672 000 in the armed forces, 289 000 civilians in Manchuria, Korea, and the Pacific, and another 509 000 in air-raids.

It was ironic, too, that this day, 15 August, the day of surrender, was traditionally revered as a day of great victory. In 1281 the great Mogul emperor, Kublai Khan, grandson of Jenghis Khan, attacked Japan with a huge invasion fleet. But on 15 August a typhoon struck Hakata Bay off Kyushu Island, crushing the Mongol boats together or piling them like matchwood on the northern peninsula. For the Japanese that wind was no ordinary wind: it was *kamikaze*, a divine wind. How cruel fate can be: for one age a day symbolizes victory, for another defeat.

The people in front of the Imperial Palace cried out, 'What a wonderful blessing it is that Tenno himself can call on us and we can hear his own voice in person. We are thoroughly satisfied in such a great sacrifice.' Part of the crowd broke into a storage shed and got drunk on stocks of rice wine, or on *suri* and *duburoku*, illegal, home-made brews. Others burst into tears; many beat the ground in despair with their burned fists. The majority simply slipped away silently, resigned to their fate. Without a single word of protest, without firing another shot, the war ended, providing the greatest example of discipline history has ever witnessed. Suddenly the Japanese people had to make a complete about face and be willing to surrender unconditionally. And this they did – because the Emperor had commanded it.

For the Japanese the Emperor was God and therefore invincible. Then suddenly had come the unconditional surrender and the Emperor said 'I am not God' – a total material and spiritual rupture. The missionaries had never accepted the Emperor as God. And for this they were persecuted and imprisoned and sometimes executed. But now they defended the Emperor. 'He is not God, but he is the representative of God, he holds the authority; you must follow him.'

For many thousands of emaciated Allied prisoners of war this day of surrender, 15 August, was a day of particular humiliation and suffering as they were subjected to the angry resentment and *kataki* (revenge) of their guards. For some American crewmen who had recently baled out over Kyushu it was their last day. In a squalid act of vengeance sixteen of them were hacked to pieces by officers of Western Headquarters Command. Nor was any attention paid to the cease-fire by the Red Army forces, who continued their advance through Manchuria to the 38th parallel on the Korean peninsula.

For everyone at the Novitiate, however, the day was one of great celebration. Not only because the war had ended, but because it was the Feast of the Assumption of Our Lady, and also the 400th anniversary of the first Jesuit missionary setting foot on Japanese soil – Saint Francis Xavier, the former Basque aristocrat, who landed on Kagoshima on 15 August 1549.

part three

The After Years

Chapter Eleven

Radiation sickness

Some days after the Hiroshima and Nagasaki bombings a strange, new illness seemed to be attacking the survivors of the bombs. They called it *muyoku-ganbo* (a weariness with living). They believed it was due to 'breathing poison' caused by the atomic blasts. Father Arrupe described the phenomenon.

Many who were in the city at the moment of the explosion and had suffered no apparent injuries whatsoever, but who, nevertheless, after a few days felt weak and came to us saying they felt a terrible interior heat, that perhaps they had inhaled a poisonous gas ... and in a short time they were dead.

The first case occurred for me when I was treating an elderly man for two deep wounds on his back. A man came to me and said: 'Please, Father, come to my house because my son tells me he has a very bad sore throat.'

Since the man I was treating was gravely ill, I answered: 'It's probably a cold. Give him some aspirin and make him perspire; you'll see he'll get well.' Within two hours the boy died.

Later a girl of thirteen came weeping and said: 'Father, look what's happening to me.'

And opening her mouth, she showed me bleeding gums, small sores on the lining of the mouth and an acute pharyngitis. She showed me too how her hair was falling out in her hands in bunches. In two days she was dead.

After some investigations and studying a few cases, we found the following symptoms: a destruction of all parts of the composition of the blood, medulla, spleen, lymphatic gangliae and capillaries: that is, a typical case of radioactive attack. Knowing the cause, we were able by means of blood transfusions etc., to help these poor victims and save some lives.*

The first stage had been all over before the doctors even knew they were dealing with a new sickness. That was direct bombardment of the body by the gamma and other rays produced by the nuclear

---

* Arrupe, Pedro, SJ, 'Surviving the Atom Bomb', in *Recollections and Reflections of Pedro Arrupe, SJ*.

fission of the bomb. These were the seemingly uninjured people who had died suddenly and so mysteriously in the first few hours or days of the bomb. This massive dose of radiation had killed 95 per cent of the people within half a mile of the bomb's explosion and many thousands of people who were farther away. For those who weren't killed instantly, the rays would cause the nuclei of the body cells to degenerate and break the cell walls. Their mauve lips would open and close like the gills of a fish as those affected struggled for breath. Then a tremor would pass through their bodies, a rattle would come from their throats and they would be dead.

There were thousands of others who did not die immediately who succumbed later to what was called 'radiation sickness' or the dreadful 'atomic disease'. These were the delayed-action victims of the bomb. The second stage of the strange, new disease, set in about ten or fifteen days later, with nausea and vomiting, headache, malaise, fever, bleeding and diarrhoea. The first symptom of this stage was falling hair: whole tufts would be dislodged from the scalp while brushing the hair. Eyebrows would also fall out. Then chill and fever, sometimes as high as 106 degrees. The bones ached continually. Then diarrhoea, which was most unfortunate and disconcerting as the government ration of toilet paper was twelve sheets per family per week.

Doctors did not know what the disease was, although they guessed that it was somehow connected with *shi no hai* (death ashes) as they called radiation fall-out. Since the true nature of the 'new' disease was not known patients were usually wrongly diagnosed and given the wrong treatment. Thus patients with fever and diarrhoea and the passage of blood were often diagnosed as suffering from dysentery and sent to an infirmary for infectious diseases. In any case there were no known remedies for the sickness.

The third stage, about twenty-five to thirty days after the bomb, involved blood disorders: gums would bleed, the white blood cell count would drop dramatically, and bright red or purple spots would appear all over the body and mucous membranes. The drop in the number of white blood corpuscles reduced a patient's capacity to resist infection; open wounds were unusually slow in healing, sore throats and mouths would develop. The two key parameters that made the difference between life and death were the fever and the white blood cell count. If the fever remained high and steady the chances of survival were slim. The white cell count always dropped below 4000 (the normal count is between 5000 and 7000). But if it fell below 1000 there was little chance of life. If the patient did survive this stage anaemia, or a drop in the red blood count, would occur.

A fourth stage was the reaction that set in as the body struggled to compensate for its ills, as, for instance, when the white count not only returned to normal but increased to much higher levels than normal. Many patients would succumb at this stage, through infections in the chest cavity etc. What caused further complications to those with radiation sickness was the prevalence of the debilitating roundworm parasite. Due to a shortage of chemical fertilizers night soil was used on a wide scale as a substitute and the roundworm parasites flourished in the night soil.

One of those to succumb to 'radiation sickness' was the Methodist pastor, Mr Tanimoto, who had done such sterling work in ferrying the wounded across the river from Asano Park. Tanimoto had a high fever. There was an ancient Japanese treatment for fever. Father Kleinsorge showed his colleague how to administer to himself moxibustion. He placed a twist of the stimulant herb *moxa* on the pastor's wrist, where the pulse could be felt, and then set alight the twist. He found that each moxa treatment temporarily reduced his fever by one degree. He also tried Japanese *kyu* treatments and took as much vitamin C as he could get.

Towards the end of August, Father Kleinsorge himself became ill. He complained of feeling weak and faint. The injuries he had sustained but made nothing of were now swollen and inflamed. He was running a fever of 104 degrees. He was seriously anaemic; his white cell blood count was only 3000.

You would have thought Hiroshima had suffered enough. But no. What man had not finished off, nature strove to do. On 17 September what remained of the flattened city was hit by a typhoon – the *Makurazaki*. Being so low-lying, encircled by the two main arms of the seven-mouthed River Ohta, the delta lands of Hiroshima were always susceptible to flooding whenever the river overflowed its banks. Almost every other year the water roaring down from the mountains after the rainy season would break the dykes and in bad years this would coincide with mountainous seas, whipped up by typhoons, pouring into the areas below sea level. On the 17th, just over a month after the surrender, there was a cloudburst. By afternoon the torrential rains and 100 knot winds from the East China Sea had increased to hurricane intensity. It increased in strength hour by hour until midnight when, in the pitch blackness, it flattened the newly-built shacks and hovels in which the helpless survivors of the atom bomb were eking out some kind of existence.

The flood waters took over from where the bomb had left off; they swept away many bridges that had survived the Thin Man's blast, they undermined the foundations of the few buildings that still stood;

the streets were raging torrents. Ten miles to the west, the Ono Army Hospital stood amid beautiful pines on a mountain-side and a team of experts from Kyoto Imperial University were studying the delayed-action effects of radiation sickness. Suddenly the hospital slid down the mountain into the Inland Sea, drowning everybody, investigators and patients alike. The flood waters destroyed half of the city's bridges that had survived, leaving the people with only boats to cross the Ohta's seven branches. Since most of the city's policemen and firemen had been killed in the atomic blast five weeks earlier there was no organization left to rescue the hapless victims of the typhoon.

The surrender ceremonies took place on the US battleship *Missouri* on 2 September 1945. The American Occupation troops moved into Hiroshima on 10 October. General MacArthur had set up his *Dai-Ichi*, or headquarters, in Tokyo. He was to be assisted in his work of governance by the Japanese Liberal Democratic Party which supported American policies.

In Sugamo Prison in Tokyo, which until recently had held Allied prisoners of war, the Japanese so-called 'war criminals' were incarcerated, awaiting trial on charges of initiating and profiting from the war. Among these was General Hideki Tojo, who was Prime Minister for most of the time of World War II and under whose direction Japan had gained her early smashing victories in Asia and the Pacific. He still nursed a bullet wound in his chest resulting from a suicide attempt. Not for nothing was he nicknamed 'Razor'. Eventually Tojo was found guilty by MacArthur's International Military Tribunal for the Far East and hanged. But there were many Japanese – and others – who felt it was those who had developed and used the atomic bombs who were the real war criminals.

After the bombings of Hiroshima and Nagasaki, the scientists responsible were treated like gods for their magnificent, almost godlike, achievements. Robert Oppenheimer, the 'father of the atom bomb', was treated like a victorious commander-in-chief. He was regarded as a man whose miraculous weapon had spared the country the dreaded prospect of enormous casualties in the invasion of the Japanese mainland; but also as a kind of peace-maker whose amazing achievement would make all wars superfluous, too horrendous ever to contemplate. (Indeed, there has been no war between the super-powers since those awful days of August 1945.) The Marines on the tiny island of Tinian were particularly glad because they were to bear the brunt, as front line troops, of the forthcoming landing in Tokyo Bay.

But there were many whose pangs of conscience pricked as 'collaborators, even brilliant collaborators, with death.' The German physicist Otto Hahn could not bear to think that it was his researches, undertaken without any idea of their practical exploitation as weapons of war, that had eventually led to the deaths of hundreds of thousands of men, women and children. After the surrender of Germany in 1945 he and other prominent nuclear scientists were arrested, mainly to prevent the Russians getting their hands on them first. After arrest by the Alsos Mission he was taken by way of Heidelberg and the American Special Transit Camp, known as the 'Dustbin', near Paris, to an English country house, Farm Hall, in Godmanchester, near Cambridge. He was in British custody when he heard of the bombings of Hiroshima and Nagasaki and the horrendous consequences of the studies he had completed nearly seven years before. So secretly had Hahn been taken out of Germany that even the Swedish Academy that wished to propose him for the Nobel Prize for Chemistry, could not find him.

When Hahn first learned of the terrible consequences of atomic fission he became very depressed and his colleagues feared he would take his life. 'Watch Hahn!' they whispered to one another. In the diary of Dr Bagge, one of those interned – or rather kept in safe custody – with Hahn, for 7 August 1945 he writes:

At 2 a.m. there was a knock on our door and in came von Laue. 'We have to do something, I am very worried about Otto Hahn. This news has upset him dreadfully, and I fear the worst.' We stayed up for quite a while and only when we had made sure Hahn had fallen asleep did we go to bed.

After Hiroshima and Nagasaki Einstein became one of the most resolute of those scientists opposed to the atom bomb, the 'hell weapon'.

For a time Hiroshima had no municipal government at all. Mayor Kuriya had been killed or was missing. In November a new municipal government was set up under the direction of the Allied Military Government. There were a few rooms in the Town Hall that had not been totally destroyed. There were a few walls standing, askew and blackened by fire; the floors, where any existed, were uneven. Undeterred, the new municipal government moved in in November and began the task of rebuilding the city. In the winter they would sit, huddled in overcoats, hats on, burning any rubbish they could find for warmth, while the snow flurried in.

Painfully slowly, but resolutely, the work of rebuilding began. A few trams appeared on the main route, a few on the Miyajima route, along with a few buses. As the years went by, monuments arose to the events of 1945. In 1950 the Catholic Cathedral of Peace was built. In August 1952 the Memorial to the Atomic Victims was dedicated. It was made of granite, with a simple roof structure in the style of the old Japanese houses. The inscription on it reads:

Rest in peace. The mistake shall never be made again.

The monument stands like the skeleton of some weird monster that had once come and devoured one third of Hiroshima's people and knocked down nine tenths of its buildings.

The Children's Peace Monument is covered with paper cranes, folded by school children, in memory of the little *hibakusha* girl, victim of radiation, who, dying of leukaemia, had been told that if she folded one thousand of them, she would get better. At her six hundredth paper crane the twelve year old's strength began to ebb away. On her 644th she had to give up. Her last words were 'Please don't cry Mummy and Daddy.'

The Jesuits, too, began their rebuilding. Father Kleinsorge and his colleagues lived in tents beside the new chapel and school buildings as they rose steadily out of the ashes. In the meanwhile they improvised with 'blue sky schools', the children doing their lessons in the open air. A gigantic cedar tree refused to perish; it still smouldered weeks after the Thin Man had struck it down, a beacon of life and hope amid the sea of ruin. When the autumn rains came life became difficult; pathways, already pitted with holes and ash, would become torrents of blackish slime.

Father Kleinsorge got no better: the humming in the ears, the fainting, the tiredness, the aching bones, continued. It was decided to take him to the Catholic International Hospital in Tokyo, where the medical facilities and expertise would be better than at Hiroshima. Father Arrupe and Father Cieslik took Father Kleinsorge to Kobe, where a Jesuit from Kobe took him the rest of the journey. The physician in Kobe sent a message to the Mother Superior of the International Hospital: 'Think twice before giving this man blood transfusions because with atom bomb patients we are not sure that they will stop bleeding.' (In actual fact, a blood transfusion would have been the best therapy for the priest.) Father Kleinsorge stayed in Tokyo for several weeks where he seemed to get better, before returning to Hiroshima.

At first the Japanese believed they would be treated badly by the American Occupation troops. But when they saw the GIs come down from their jeeps and play with the children, giving them sweets and chewing gum and clothing, their hatred relented. The armies of occupation, for their part, behaved honourably. This mutual collaboration was most commendable: absolute submission on the part of the Japanese on one hand and on the other, generosity and friendship on the part of the victors. American Shogun MacArthur was masterminding a military occupation that will go down as one of the most peaceful in history, the friendship between the general and the Emperor being a big factor in it. MacArthur's reforms, designed to root democracy deep into Japanese life, to make a return to militarism impossible and to restore a shattered economy, won the Japanese people's support.

In course of time Hiroshima's meagre supplies of food ran out. The rice allotment had to be replaced by a 'caloric equivalent' in rotten yams and stale barley; both inedible. People were living on grasses, seaweed and crabs' shells collected on the seashore. Fishes and little crabs were fried in oils of various sorts, even motor lubricants. The meat roasting on small spits often originated from the pound for stray dogs. Most pathetic of all was the sight of the hundreds of *furoji*, homeless orphans, living in hovels in the ghettos, the *buraki* of Minami, Misasa and Fukushima in the north, central and southern quarters, scavenging for food in the rubbish piles. At night lamps would glimmer from their ramshackle huts, smoke curling up from their rough and ready fireplaces, burning bamboo stolen from nearby temples.

The shortages brought in the thieves and the black marketeers. A rice ball cost forty times its pre-war price. No possessions were safe. Emergency letter boxes, made of wood, were broken up and carried away for firewood. The thugs of the underworld, in their tight-fitting 'Eisenhower jackets', held power in Hiroshima. The Katsugiya operated the black markets – in 'black rice', 'black fish', 'black oil', and even 'black water'. There were few taps and so the sale of water was a highly lucrative racket. There was a noticeable and steady moral and social decline among the populace. Robbery, assault, rape, murder, were everyday occurrences. '*Dorobo! Dorobo!* [Thief! Thief!]' was a shout often heard in the streets. But the pickpocket would just disappear in the crowd. The repatriation of three-quarters of a million ex-soldiers from the former empire overseas, some whole, many maimed, begging in the streets in their ragged army uniforms, didn't exactly ease the situation.

On the street corners appeared a new phenomenon – the 'butterflies', as the street girls were called. A *pan pan* girl cost a packet of cigarettes. The *ianshos* (brothels) were back in business. The young men and women became record crazy; from early morning until late at night the city reverberated to the love moans of Western crooners and to the muted saxophones of Boogie music. Music was the *hiropon* drug for youth in its pursuit of pleasure and instant satisfaction.

Pin-ball saloons abounded even though the player of *Panchinko* invariably lost.

In due course the Jesuits had built a relatively permanent three-storey mission house in Nobori-machi, like the one that had been devoured by flames. They also re-opened their kinder-garten school. Father Kleinsorge shared the pastoral duties of this mission centre with Father Laderman, every day visiting and comforting the sick, the bereaved, the poor, the homeless, in their dark, windowless, shacks made from scraps of tin roofing, and packing cases 'appropriated' from the Imperial Army. He would come home in the evening utterly exhausted. Worse than that, his wounds would not heal, he had diarrhoea, high fever, mildly fluctuating white cell blood counts and no energy. In August 1946 he was back at the Catholic International Hospital in Tokyo.

Two years later he was appointed priest in charge of the much grander church in Misasa. Apart from saying Mass each day for his congregation, and visiting the *hibakusha*, as the victims of the atom bomb were called, he would be occupied with teaching and with giving retreats to aspiring novices and others and with ministering to the nuns of the Convent of Helpers of Holy Souls attached to the church. He would even baby-sit for young mothers. He would often take the one-hour train journey to Saijyo to comfort the TB patients at the sanatorium there. Tuberculosis was widespread. In the 1940s Japan had the highest TB ratio among the developed countries.

One day a parishioner asked him to visit a friend of hers, a Buddhist, who was morbid and very depressed. He duly arrived at the hospital He still felt shock and revulsion at what he saw. The *hibakusha*, the atom- lepers, with their 'devil' faces, were much in evidence – horribly ugly, covered with *keloids*, thick, itching, rubbery, copper-red, crab-like scars that had formed over their burns. (The word keloid derives from the Greek word *chele* meaning a crab's claw, which it resembles.) One young girl had an eruption of scar tissue that spurted out of her left cheek, flowing like lava down the side of her face, over her jaw and into her shoulder. Another had angry purple welts that tore along both sides of her face in cleaving sweeps from nose to ear. They all looked away to hide their hideous disfigurements. Little boys and girls with balding heads stepped between the straw mats waving the stumps of what remained of their arms. The right eye-lid of a little girl had been seared away. Left uncovered, the eye watered permanently as though possessed of a special grief of its own.

He was taken to the *futon*, a quilt mattress, on which a young girl sat, dressed in a blue kimono, tight across her legs and wearing *getas*, wooden sandals. She sat in the formal *seiza* style, with her back straight and her insteps and feet flattened underneath her buttocks.

'*Konnichi wa* [Good day],' he greeted her.

She was Miss Toshiko Sasaki, the young lady who had worked in the personnel department of the East Asia Tin Works at Kannonmachi, who had hoped to give her sick baby brother Akio, the present of a *dharma* doll. She had not done so – because *Pika-Don* intervened. She came straight to the point with the priest.

'If your God is so good and kind, how can he let people suffer like this?' she asked, as she gestured to her shrunken leg, to the deformed patients around her, and with a sweep of her angry hand, to the nuclear ashscape that was around her.

He let her go on. He let her tell what happened to her on that frightful morning of 6 August.

She had just settled herself in at her desk at the East Asia Tin Works when the room was filled with a blinding, slightly vermilion, light. A blast of hot air from outside smacked her face and slammed her sideways. The blast ripped through the building. For a moment time appeared to stop. Then the whole world seemed to fall in. The wooden floor above her collapsed in splinters and fell in on her, along with timbers, tiles and corrugated iron – and people. Fragments of glass flew about like leaves in a whirlwind. The book-cases behind her toppled on to her and crushed her left leg. The room went black, as if the sun had set, and she lost consciousness. She was wholly unconscious (she later estimated) for about three hours. There was tremendous pain in her broken horribly twisted, left leg. It was so black under the books and debris that the borderline between awareness and unconsciousness was fine; she must have crossed it several times, for the pain seemed to come and go. At the moments when it was sharpest, she felt that her leg had been cut off somewhere below the knee. Later, she heard someone walking on top of the wreckage above her, and anguished voices called out, evidently from within the devastation around her: 'Please help! Get us out!'

People began digging. She had a bookcase and an iron beam over her. A man started helping to get her out but when he saw the size of the task walked away, saying 'You'll have to get yourself out.'

Eventually other people did dig her out. Her leg was broken and cut and hung askew below her knee. For two whole days and two whole nights she lay in the courtyard of the East Asia Tin Works. During the day the sun burned down out of a cloudless sky on to the dusty, treeless city. When the wind rose the stench of decay intensified. At night she shivered with cold. She had not a drop of water to drink or a morsel to eat. She wondered what had happened to her family, to her baby brother Akio. The pain in her broken leg made sleep impossible. A man had placed her under a corrugated iron lean to. The man who had done this act of kindness had also placed two horribly wounded persons beside her – a woman with her whole breast sheared off and a man, his face all raw from burns. They were covered with flies. Maggots crawled in and out of the wounds. The smell was horrible. Her own leg by now was putrefied. Her only diversion came when men arrived at the factory air-raid shelter and began to haul corpses out of it with ropes. On 8 August she was found by some friends. They told her the Tamura Paediatric Hospital had been totally destroyed – along with her mother and baby brother Akio.

She was seen by two Army doctors who diagnosed that gas gangrene had set into her leg. Amputation of the leg was the only solution. But they had no equipment. So she was put on a launch and taken to the nearby island of Ninoshima, where there was a military hospital. The doctors there found no evidence of gangrene. She was then taken to Hatsukaichi, a town several miles south west of Hiroshima, where the primary school had been converted to a hospital. A rubber pipe was inserted into the wound to drain the putrescence. She had a compound fracture of the left tibia, with swelling of the lower left leg. But there was no plaster of Paris. She was given aspirin for her fever. By now spot haemorrhages had erupted on her skin.

She was next taken, on a mat, to the Red Cross Hospital in Hiroshima. This hospital, just a mile south of where the bomb detonated, lost 80 per cent of its staff, including 408 student nurses, on that fatal day. Toshiko couldn't get over how the flowers and vegetation had grown, even luxuriated. The bluets and Spanish bayonets, the morning glory, lilies, sesame, panic grass, feverfew, hair-fruited bean, were in blossom. The sickle senna was everywhere, among the bricks and even through the cracks in the asphalt – as if a load of it had been dropped with the Thin Man. Weeds were sprouting from the foundations of houses. It was as if the gamma radiation, whilst destroying the blood cells of the human body, had given extra nourishment to the plants. Where there was water the lotus bloomed. The lotus was the emblem of Hiroshima. It always held a pride of place in Buddhism. Because it will flourish even in stinking swamps it was chosen as the symbol of the compassionate Buddha who brings goodness from corrupt human hearts.

She enjoyed seeing the yellow-green bamboo. It was the ideal of Japanese women to be like the bamboo – graceful, gentle, sensitive, strong. The slightest wind will stir the bamboo's filigree leaves but even the autumn typhoons won't uproot it. While the giant cedar and the cypress will be uprooted after a storm, the slender bamboo will stand serene. The bamboo was the symbol of endurance and fidelity. No matter how cold the winter, or how torrid the summer, the bamboo remains green and vigorous.

Toshiko told Father Kleinsorge about her former fiancé. When he came back from the war in China it was clear to both of them that marriage was out of the question. In fact he had never even visited her. Moreover, his parents did not want him to marry a *hibakusha*, an atom cripple.

There was much discrimination against those who had been injured by the atom bomb. They were ostracized from society. Matrimonial bureaux, which arranged most of the marriages in Japan, informed applicants from Hiroshima and Nagasaki that survivors of *Pika-Don* were not eligible, on the grounds that they might father or give birth to deformed children. Parents forbade their children who were coming up to marriageable age to play with *hibakusha* children in case they formed attachments. Public bathing establishments refused entry to men and women whose bodies were disfigured by large, ugly keloids – it was rumoured the scars were infectious. People on whom 'the devil's claws' had left their traces could not find employment.

Some years afterwards the Reverend Mr Tanimoto, the Methodist pastor whom Father Kleinsorge had known well ever since their acquaintance in Asano Park the day the bomb fell, began giving Bible classes to a group of girls whose faces had been disfigured by keloids. Later, some of them were taken, as so-called 'Hiroshima Maidens', to the United States for plastic surgery.

Father Kleinsorge himself was suffering from the effects of gamma-ray radiation. At that moment he felt ill and nauseous. He would have liked to go home to rest. But he felt he must offer the young lady some response to her question – a question which not only she, but everyone in the wider world, was asking. Otherwise she would think there was no answer to the problem of suffering.

He paused some time before answering. Then he began, 'Yes, in a sense you are right.'

He explained that, confronted with our human freedom God decided to make himself 'impotent'. He could manifest Himself to us as some clearly visible, awesome, mighty Power, claiming the abject adoration of His creatures. Instead, He gave us freedom, a free will. We can choose to worship and adore Him, or just ignore Him. Even deny His existence. He is paying for the great gift He has bestowed on us. It is precisely by giving us this gift of free will, by making us rational and free, that He has made himself impotent. He places Himself under the judgement of man who asks provocative questions of Him. We set ourselves up as the unbending judge of God's actions. We order him to justify Himself before our tribunal.

'You are so right,' he said again. 'Our world is full of suffering. How could a merciful Father, a God who is meant to be Love itself, allow such pain and agony? Is a God who permits all this truly Love?'

He told her that this same merciful Father allowed His own Son to die an agonizing death on the Cross. How can that be? The question rather is how could it *not* be? How could God justify Himself before human history, so full of human misery, without subjecting the Son He loved so much to ignomy and agony too. The crucified Christ is the proof of God's solidarity with man in his suffering, of His great love for us. God's omnipotence is manifested precisely in the fact that He freely accepted suffering. He could have chosen otherwise. He didn't. He chose rather to show His love by coming as a man who would endure the most horrendous insults and pain and even die. Suffering is an evil. But God did not want it. He did not make it. We do. Jesus Christ made it a means of sanctification.

'Yes,' he concluded. 'God is all-loving and omnipotent. His wisdom and omnipotence are placed, by free choice, at the service of creation.'

It was time to go.

'*Sayonara* [farewell],' the priest said and with a low bow left the ward.

Father Kleinsorge made a point of visiting the young lady whenever he could. He noticed she was becoming less and less depressed. She was even asking questions about what was happening in the world outside her hospital. In due course, she was discharged from hospital and went to live in her house in the suburb of Koi.

Father Kleinsorge continued to visit her in Koi. Eventually she began work at the White Chrysanthemum Orphanage, looking after young girls, some of whom had previously been living alone in houses inhabited by gangsters and prostitutes.

One day she explained that over the months she had experienced *satori*. *Satori* was an ancient and revered Zen word meaning spiritual awakening, enlightenment, that comes like 'the flash of a sword cutting through the problems of existence.' She asked to be given instruction in the teachings of the Church. He was overcome with delight when she eventually asked to be received into the Church. But when the time came it was Father Cieslik who baptized her: Father Kleinsorge was back in hospital in Tokyo.

Father Kleinsorge spent time in and out of hospital in Tokyo. Part of the problem was that he was slowly killing himself, doing too much for others. He imbibed to the full the Japanese spirit of *enryo* – setting the self apart, putting the wishes of others first. When gifts of delicacies came from relatives in Germany, he gave them all away. When he got penicillin from an Occupation doctor, he gave it to parishioners who were not as sick as he. He continued to give lessons on the catechism when he had a high fever. After he came back from a long hike of pastoral calls, the Misasa housekeeper would see him collapse on the steps of his rectory, head down – a figure, it seemed, of utter defeat. The next day, he would be out in the streets again.

Gradually, over years of this unremitting labour, he gathered his modest harvest: some four hundred baptisms, some forty marriages. Everything seemed worth the toil and effort and suffering when one day his housekeeper told him he had a visitor. He opened the door of the modest presbytery house. On the *genkan* (front porch) stood a young lady. She bowed so low in the traditional Japanese fashion that her long black locks fell over her hands.

'*Shinspu-sama* [Father], I would like to become a nun,' Miss Toshiko Sasaki said.

He was speechless.

The housekeeper produced a pot of *ocha* (thin green tea). Father Kleinsorge suggested the Helpers of the Holy Souls, who had a convent in Misasa, looking after the poor and doing home nursing.

The Japanese girl again bowed low before taking her leave. In 1957 Toshiko took her vows of poverty, chastity and obedience and became Sister Dominique Sasaki. She was now thirty-three years old. Straight from the Novitiate Sister Dominique was sent as Director of a Home for seventy old people near Kurosaki, on the island of Kyushu.

Most of the old men were former miners from the notoriously cruel Kyushu mines. She was to work there for twenty years. Her greatest gift, she found, was her ability to help the inmates die in peace. She would speak little, but would hold a hand or touch an arm, simply to let the person know she was there. Being as near to death herself when the Thin Man devastated Hiroshima, she knew what peace meant to the dying. When, in 1980, she celebrated twenty-five years as a nun and she was presented with a picture of the Virgin Mary, she commented: 'It is as if I had been given a spare life when I survived the atom-bomb. But I prefer not to look back. I shall keep moving forward.'

While Miss Toshiko Sasaki was changing her name to Sister Dominique, Father Kleinsorge SJ was changing his to Father Takakura SJ. Father Kleinsorge loved the Japanese and their ways. One of his German colleagues, Father Berzikofer, jokingly said that Father Kleinsorge was married to Japan.

Shortly after Father Kleinsorge moved to the Misasa church, he read that a new law on naturalization had been passed by the Diet, with these requirements: that one live in Japan for at least five years, be over twenty years old and mentally sound, be of good character, be able to support oneself, and be able to accept single nationality. He hastened to submit proofs that he met all these, and after some months of review he was accepted. He registered himself as a Japanese citizen under the name he would henceforth bear: Father Makoto Takakura.

For a few months in the spring and summer of 1956, his poor health declining still further, Father Takakura filled a temporary vacancy in a small parish in the Boborimachi district. One of the Hiroshima Maidens, Tomoko Nakabayashi, whom Father Takakura had converted and baptized, had died on an operating table at Mount Sinai Hospital in New York, during attempted plastic surgery. Her ashes were carried to her family when the first group of Maidens returned to Hiroshima that summer of 1956, and it fell to Father Takakura to preside at her funeral. During it, he nearly fainted, he was so ill.

Gradually Father Takakura's ailments grew so bad that in 1957 he had to enter the rebuilt Hiroshima Red Cross Hospital. He stayed there for a whole year. His most disturbing complaint was a weird infection in his fingers, which had become bloated with pus and would not heal. He had fever and 'flu-like symptoms. His white blood count was seriously low, and he had pain in his knees, particularly the left one, and in other joints. His fingers were operated on and slowly healed. He was treated for leukopenia. Before his discharge, an ophthalmologist found that he had the beginnings of a cataract due to gamma ray radiation.

He returned to the large Misasa congregation, but it was harder and harder for him to carry the kind of overload he cherished. Dragged down by constant pain and by infections that were abetted by his shortage of white cells, he limped through his days, pushing himself beyond his strength.

Finally, in 1961, he was mercifully put out to pasture by the diocese, in a tiny church in the country town of Mukaihara. The compound of the Mukaihara church, at the crest of a steep rise from the town, enclosed a small chapel, with an oaken table for the altar and with space for a flock of about twenty to kneel, Japanese-fashion, on a spread of *tatami* matting; and, uphill, a cramped presbytery. Father Takakura chose as his bedroom a room no more than six feet square and as bare as a monk's cell; he ate in another such cell, next to it; and the kitchen and bathroom, beyond, were dark, chilly, sunken rooms, no larger than the others. Across a narrow corridor running the length of the building were an office and a much larger bedroom, which Father Takakura, true to his nature, reserved for guests.

He had builders add two rooms to the chapel and started in them what he called the St Mary's Kindergarten. So began a bleak life for four Catholics: the priest, two Japanese nuns to teach the children, and a Japanese woman to cook. Few believers came to church. His parish consisted of four previously converted families, about ten worshippers in all. Some Sundays, no one showed up for Mass.

After its first spurt, Father Takakura's energy rapidly flagged. Once each week, he took a train to Hiroshima and went to the Red Cross Hospital for a checkup. At Hiroshima station, he picked up what he loved best to read as he travelled – timetables with schedules of trains going all over Honshu Island. The doctors injected steroids into his painful joints.

In the village of Mukaihara he tried to be as inconspicuous as possible – as Japanese as he could be – *Nihon-teku*. Not wanting to be seen as high-living, he never bought meat in the local market. Meat was a luxury. But he would sometimes smuggle some out from the city, on his occasional visits there.

In 1966 the cook who had served him well had to leave. Satsue Yoshiki, a thirty-five year old, recently cured of TB and also recently baptized, took her place, acting as part-mother, part-daughter. Despite his occasional cranky temper Satsue nursed him tenderly.

One day in 1976 he slipped on the steep, icy, path leading down to the town. From then on he was bed-ridden. Yoshiki-san fed him and nursed him. He read the Bible – and the railway timetables. According to him, these were 'the only two texts that didn't tell lies'. He could tell you what train to take where, the price of food in the dining car, where to change to save money. One day he called out to Yoshiki-san, greatly excited. He had found an error in the time-table. Only the Bible held the truth!

Father Takakura got weaker and weaker. His fellow priests moved him to a two-room house in a hollow just below the Novitiate in Nagatsuka. He seldom opened his eyes. Yoshiki-san fed him only on ice-cream. When visitors came he could only say '*Arigato* [thank you]'. He went into a coma and died on 17 November 1977. At his funeral a river of severe black kimonos stretched for miles behind the coffin, softened by the white veils of the Catholic women.

He was laid to rest in a serene pine grove at the top of the hill above the Novitiate. There are always fresh flowers on the grave of Father Takakura.

Chapter Twelve

High treason

On a drab, grey, windy, winter afternoon in January 1944, a man walked along a street on lower East Side, in New York City. He was thin and sallow-complexioned, with stooping shoulders, well-wrapped against the cold. He took off his round, horned-rimmed spectacles and wiped the thick lenses. The wisps of receding hair above his wide, bulging forehead, fluttered in the wind. He put on his spectacles again. The sensitive, inquiring face, with its mildly lost air which held a great appeal, especially to women, looked up at the sign. He walked in leisurely fashion to the street corner, a tennis ball in his left hand. A strange thing to do, especially for someone who was not particularly adept at the game. But that was what he had been told to do. Nonchalantly he waited for Raymond. He had never before met this Raymond, but the man would be carrying a book with a green binding and wearing a pair of gloves, with an additional pair of gloves in his hand. How strange! Why an additional pair?

Ah, there he was. A man approached. He was about forty years old and about five feet ten inches tall, of broad build, with a smile on his round face. The two men greeted one another, then took a taxi to a restaurant on lower Third Avenue. They talked of this and that and arranged to meet again. Raymond picked up his book, along with a package of papers, and headed down the street. He turned a corner where he bumped into an acquaintance. But the two didn't speak. The acquaintance took the package of papers and disappeared into the maze of New York's streets. Raymond wandered into a subway station and jumped on a train as its doors were closing. A few stops later he suddenly jumped out, again as the doors were closing. He did this a few times before finally reaching home.

Two months later, in March, the two men met again – in Madison Avenue. But this was hardly a meeting: the two were together less than a minute. They took a few steps together into a side street. Raymond took delivery of some papers and then left. They met again in June, first at Woodside, Queens, and later in the month near Borough Hall in Brooklyn. Again there was barely time to pass the time of day. But, at last, in mid July they met at 96th Street and Central Park West and were able to enjoy a leisurely hour and a half strolling in the park.

Early in 1945 the two met again at Cambridge, just outside Boston. They agreed to see each other again six months later on the first Saturday in June 1945, at 4.00 p.m. on the Castillo Street Bridge in Santa Fé. Raymond was the first to arrive. He had an hour and a half to while away. He made his way to the museum and bought a map of the city. This way he could make his own way round the tourist spots. A few minutes after four a dilapidated old Buick rattled down Alameda Street. Raymond went forward to meet the Englishman with the thick horn-rimmed lenses and mildly lost air.

They spent half an hour together and then Raymond, a packet of papers under his arm, went off by bus to Albuquerque while the Englishman jumped into his car and chugged off in the opposite direction.

They met again on 19 September, as arranged, by a church on the road leading out of Santa Fé. The Englishman drove his old Buick to a nearby bluff overlooking the city. More and more city lights began blinking through the haze of dusk. This meeting was a long one, and the last, for the Englishman was returning to his home country.

Having returned home to England in June 1946, he had the chance of meeting, early in 1947 – not Raymond, but an associate of his. He walked into the Nag's Wood public house at Wood Green in north London and made for the saloon bar. He was carrying a copy of the weekly *Tribune*. He sat on a particular bench and ordered a whisky. He casually gazed around, then lazily began to read the front page of his paper. Occasionally he would glance up. A man took a seat not far from him. He was carrying a red book. He carried on reading. The man ordered a drink and opened his book. The two didn't so much as pass the time of day between them. Presently the man with the red book shut the pages closed, emptied his glass and walked out. The other man continued with the front page of the Tribune for a while, drained his glass and walked out. The man with the red book was some distance down the street. Eventually he caught up with him, exchanged a few words and a packet, and continued on.

In the summer of 1949 an American B-29 flying over Asian waters detected radioactive matter in the atmosphere. The Russians had obviously exploded an atom bomb, years prior to expectations. The Soviet Union simply did not have the knowledge or expertise or capability to make an atom bomb on her own resources. Someone must have given them the information they needed. Just prior to this US intelligence suspected there had been a leak of details about the atomic bomb and its construction. The suspicion was that the leak had come from one of the British scientists involved in the Manhattan Project in 1945. But who? There had been 38 British scientists involved. Where did one begin?

So MI5 began to investigate them all, yet again. Mr Skardon from MI5 visited the Atomic Energy Research Establishment in Harwell one day in December 1949. Opposite him sat the Deputy Chief Scientific Officer at the Establishment. The two went over the same old questions, the same old answers. It all seemed such a pointless waste of time. Then suddenly Skardon interjected, quite out of the blue.

'And that was when you passed secrets to a Soviet Agent.'

He looked at the other man. If he really was the guilty man his expression would give him away.

A small tip of tongue appeared between the Scientific Officer's lips, only momentarily. He paused and then replied coolly.

'No, I don't think so.' He smiled at Skardon.

He hadn't admitted anything. Yet he hadn't denied anything very categorically. His facial expression didn't give anything away. This was understandable if he was not guilty. And, if he was guilty, perhaps he had rehearsed many, many times, just such a response for just such a grilling.

The investigations of MI5 continued.

It was a cold day: 1 March 1950. The Englishman, looking thin and pale, in a suit that appeared too big for him, sat on a wooden chair, his hand resting on the arm of the chair. A big man, with a suit that looked too tight for him, sat alongside. The two men rose as Mr Derek Curtis-Bennett entered the room. Mr Curtis-Bennett, dressed in a long black gown, a white wig on his head began.

'We have done our best, but there is no hope. I fear the maximum penalty.'

The prisoner's lips parted ever so slightly.

'You know what the maximum penalty is?' the senior defence counsel asked.

The brown eyes of the balding prisoner looked up through thick lenses at Curtis-Bennett and nodded. He knew. Death by hanging.

There was some chattering of voices and the man in the too-tight suit led his prisoner up from the cells of the Old Bailey to the main court-room. The prisoner was a man of calm composure but even he was somewhat moved by the occasion. He stood there, a faint blue shadow covering his set mouth and slightly weak chin. He looked all the world like the proverbial absent-minded professor. The room was full of gowned and bewigged gentlemen. The public gallery was full to bursting. Even the Duchess of Kent and some other notables were there. Everyone rose as the Lord Chief Justice, Lord Goddard, in scarlet and ermine and preceded by a sword-bearer and the mace-bearer in their medieval costumes, entered and took his seat under the sword of Justice. The prisoner looked at the Chief Justice's table. He could not see a black cap. Perhaps that was kept in a drawer in the desk until later in the proceedings.

The Clerk of the Court rose. He turned to the dock. 'Will the prisoner rise.'

'Your name please.'

In a firm, clear, voice the prisoner replied: 'Fuchs, Klaus Fuchs.'

'And your occupation?'

'I am – was – deputy Chief Scientific Officer at the Atomic Energy Research Establishment, Harwell.'

'Klaus Fuchs, you are charged with communicating information contrary to the Official Secrets Act, 1911, and the particulars are that on days to be noted presently, for a purpose prejudicial to the safety and interest of the State, you communicated to persons to be named presently information which was calculated to be or might be useful to an enemy. Are you guilty or not guilty?'

Fuchs turned to the Chief Justice. 'Guilty, my Lord.'

Sir Hartley Shawcross, the Attorney-General, acting for the Crown, called only one witness, William James Skardon, who had obtained the confession of Fuchs. Skardon had investigated William Joyce, Lord Haw Haw, who had worked for the Nazis in Berlin during the War, and other traitors.

Skardon began with a brief biography of Fuchs. He had been born in Germany on 29 December 1911. His father was a Protestant parson. He went to Kiel University. It was in the spring of 1933 that the Nazis began to persecute the Jews and Communists. The prisoner himself had been beaten by the Nazi bully boys. He vowed to take revenge. In the universities the left-wing became popular. Impressionable students looked to the Soviet Republic and Marxist Socialism as the one hope in an increasingly impossible world. The Fascists had to be destroyed. Communism was the obvious weapon to defeat the persecutors.

Fuchs became leader of the student Communist group and fought the Nazi storm-troopers on the streets of Kiel. Like Karl Marx earlier, he came to England as a German refugee, hardened and bitter, hungry, penniless, unable to speak the language. In 1937 he obtained a PhD in mathematical physics at Bristol University and then began research under Professor Max Born at Edinburgh. In 1943 he went to the USA as part of the British team working on the atom bomb project.

Mr Skardon then catalogued the events in the course of which Fuchs had handed over the Los Alamos secrets to Soviet secret agents. Between December 1943 and August 1944 he had, in New

York, given Harry Gold (alias Raymond) the principles and details of the gas diffusion plant at Oak Ridge, Tennessee, where uranium ore was converted into the more fissionable uranium235.

In February 1945, in Boston, he gave Gold details of the plutonium bomb, its design, method of construction, and the fact that plutonium was produced in atomic piles at Hanford in the state of Washington. He also gave details of the implosion lens (a device that explodes inwards) used in detonating the plutonium bomb. (Harry Gold procured actual drawings of the implosion lens from a David Greenglass, an American spy, who, unbeknown to Fuchs, was also working at Los Alamos on the atom bomb project.)

At the first Santa Fé rendezvous with Gold in June 1945 Fuchs informed him that the atom bomb explosion would definitely take place at Alamogorde the following month. At the second Santa Fé meeting in September 1945, beside the church, Fuchs gave details of the size of the atom bomb, an important point, what it contained, how it was constructed and how it was detonated. Fuchs also gave details of the explosion he himself had seen.

Later, in 1947, while he was working at the Atomic Research Establishment in Harwell, Fuchs passed on details of Britain's post-war atomic developments.

Fuchs pleaded guilty on all four counts.

'Do you have anything to say?'

'No, my Lord,' Fuchs replied.

Mr Curtis-Bennett, senior counsel for Fuchs, pleaded in mitigation the intense political pressure Fuchs had suffered as a youth in Nazi Germany.

There was a deathly hush as Lord Chief Justice Goddard began his summing up.

'Your statement which has been read shows to me the depth of self-deception into which people like yourself can fall.'

He paused. His hand moved towards his right-hand drawer. This, thought Fuchs, was the moment when the dreaded black cap would be withdrawn and placed on the learned Judge's head. The learned Judge continued his summing up.

'Your crime to me is only thinly differentiated from high treason, for which the penalty is death by hanging. In this country we observe rigidly the rule of law. As technically your crime is not high treason, since you did not pass information to an enemy but to an ally, so you are not tried for that offence.'

Fuchs could hardly believe his ears. All the time he had been in prison he was convinced he would hang.

The Lord Chief Justice went on.

'The maximum sentence which Parliament has ordained for your crime is fourteen years imprisonment and that is the sentence I pass upon you.'

Fuchs, thirty-eight years old, was taken from the dock, down to the cells and thence to Wormwood Scrubs Prison. He was put into prison uniform. As he was no longer a person awaiting trial, he now had no special privileges. Three months later he was taken to Stafford Gaol, where he spent his days, not doing theoretical physics, but sewing canvas mail bags.

British counter-intelligence had got their man. But what about Raymond, the man to whom Fuchs had passed his secrets? The Federal Bureau of Investigation in America dearly wanted to know. But the only lead that pointed to him was that he was a man about 40 years, of stocky build, with dark brown hair. There were millions of Americans who fitted that description.

One day in prison Fuchs had a visitor – from British counter-intelligence. He was shown a set of about twenty photographs. Was Raymond one of these? Fuchs picked out one photograph. He looked at it for a long while, his delicate fingers tapping the table, his wide forehead creased in deep furrows.

'There's something familiar about this man,' he murmured. He covered the head of the photograph to simulate a hat and stared at it for a long while. 'I cannot swear, but I am pretty sure this is the man.'

The FBI checked on the man. It finally decided the man was not Raymond; inquiries showed he could not have been Fuch's accomplice.

Several months later Fuchs was again disturbed in his sewing of mail bags with another batch of photographs from across the Atlantic. The wan prisoner squinted long and hard at the photographs of a man with a round face and bushy hair. No, Raymond was not there.

In May 1950 two special agents of the FBI entered the Philadelphia General Hospital to interview the chemist in charge of biological research there. The small chemist was happy to be interviewed. He answered questions about his earlier life. He had been born in Switzerland, and then became a naturalized American. Presently the two agents produced a picture of Dr Fuchs. The chemist just frowned, then kept on looking at the picture.

The agents were surprised when the chemist said: 'This is a very unusual picture. He is that English spy.'

How did he know? they asked. Well, his picture had been published in all the newspapers.

Had he ever seen Fuchs? No.

Had he ever met Fuchs? Certainly not.

Had he ever been to New Mexico? No. He had never been west of the Mississippi River.

The FBI agents thanked the chemist for his co-operation and left.

But they were back some days later. Could they take a few moving pictures of the man? Sure, why not?

To prove beyond any doubt that he had nothing to hide he told the agents to search his offices, even his rooms. In his presence two agents did search the house, a two-storey brick and stone row hose at 6823 Kindred Street in Philadelphia's North-east sector. The chemist suggested they start in the bedroom, where he kept his most personal papers. Whenever they found an item of interest the chemist would confidently given an explanation. They went from room to room.

'What about this?' one of the agents asked.

The chemist was startled; his mouth fell open as he stood paralysed.

'Where did that come from?' he finally said as if in a trance.

'You tell us,' the agent replied.

There was a pause.

'You said,' the agent reminded him, 'you had never been west of the Mississippi? How do you account for this?'

The chemist stared unbelieving at the Chamber of Commerce map of Santa Fé that he had bought when he first went there to find his way to the rendezvous point on the bridge without asking questions of the local inhabitants.

Facing the chemist, whose impregnable poise of an accomplished deceiver was now shattered, the agent asked, 'Would you like to tell us the whole story?'

Abruptly Harry Gold (alias Raymond) blurted out, 'I ... I am the man to whom Klaus Fuchs gave his information.'

Quite by coincidence, less than an hour before Gold's confession a cable was received at FBI Headquarters in Washington from London, saying that after seeing the moving pictures Fuchs had identified the man as Raymond, his American confederate.

Harry Gold made a full confession. He had come to America in July 1914, the three-year-old child of an immigrant family. His parents, natives of Russia, changed their name from Golodnitsky to Gold. As a youth he became entangled with atheist and communist associates and became a member of the Communist Party. To him Russia was the great 'protector of democracy' at a time when Hitler's Nazis were destroying free speech, trade unions and opposition parties and persecuting minorities. Though his parents had fled from their native land, he determined to assist Russia in its industrialization programme by passing it secrets. In promoting the

Red cause he denied himself money, luxuries, vacations, even sleep; he gave everything he had, including, finally, his honour. In his misguided idealism he stole the Western world's most important secrets to aid a tyranny far greater than Hitler's – that of the USSR. The secrets he acquired from Fuchs he passed on to Anatoli Yakovlev, the Russian vice-consul in New York. As an idealist he considered himself above the law, justifying means by ends. And the Soviet Union 'honoured' him in turn for his efforts. Oh, yes! He was awarded the Order of the Red Star. He was now entitled to free bus rides in the city of Moscow.

On 9 December 1950, Gold stood in the Federal Court in Philadelphia arraigned before Judge James P. McGranery. Gold confessed his 'terrible mistake'.

'There is a puny inadequacy about any words telling how deep and horrible is my remorse,' he declared. He thanked the Court for a fair trial and commended the authorities for their good treatment of him.

'Most certainly,' he added, 'this could never have happened in the Soviet Union.'

The Judge, who had been listening intently lifted his gavel and pronounced the sentence. 'Thirty years.'

The little, insignificant man nodded, and US deputy marshals led Gold out of the courtroom. He had sacrificed his life and jeopardized the security of his adopted country for 'free bus rides in Moscow' – a privilege which fate was never to allow him to enjoy.

While Gold was being led away, in New York State a married couple, Julius and Ethel Rosenberg, were awaiting execution for handing over atom secrets to the Russians. David Greenglass, another spy, pleaded guilty and turned State's evidence. He was sent to federal prison for fifteen years. The Rosenbergs were executed in the electric chair.

ෂ්ඬ

On 23 September, 1949, the Soviet Union announced that it had developed an atomic bomb. In October 1952 Great Britain carried out its first test of an atom bomb. In the same year the US tested a new type of nuclear explosion – the hydrogen bomb, or H-bomb. In August 1953 the Soviet Union tested its first H-bomb. In 1954 twenty-three crewmen of the fishing vessel Lucky Dragon No. 5 and its cargo of tuna were affected by radiation from the American test of an H-bomb on Bikini Atoll. On 15 May, 1957, Britain detonated an H-bomb on Christmas Island in the Indian Ocean. On 13 February 1960 France tested a nuclear device in the Sahara Desert. On 16 October 1964

China tested a nuclear weapon and on 17 June 1967, an H-bomb. On 18 May 1974 India carried out a test on a nuclear device.

And so, as the first makers of the nuclear bomb had come to fear would happen, the weapon of mass destruction began to proliferate. More and more countries were coming to own them. Since the break-up of the Soviet Union, several new republics – Ukraine, Russia, Khazakstan – own their own atomic bombs or the uranium and plutonium needed for their construction. It only needs another Hitler, another mad-man, some deranged dictator, some unscrupulous or desperate regime, to repeat the holocausts of Hiroshima and Nagasaki. Someone aboard a *Polaris* or *Trident* submarine or aboard a long-range bomber could 'take out' any number of population centres.

Fortunately for mankind, the Cold War has given way to the Cold Peace. There has been a comprehensive ban on nuclear testing. Nations are voluntarily agreeing to disband, or appreciably reduce, their stocks of total destruction weapons. They must seek sane and prudent ways to settle their differences. Security in the nuclear age rests on global interdependence, as well as on changing our own hearts. There is talk in the air of disarmament and the ultimate elimination of all war. If that happens the sacrifice of so many lives in Hiroshima and Nagasaki will not have been in vain.

Chapter Thirteen

'I was a stranger and you welcomed me'

The old man was obviously very tired and in great pain. The few wispy grey locks remaining on his head fell over one corner of his forehead. He turned his head on the pillow and looked out of the window on a warm and sunny August afternoon. Suddenly he called out. He wanted to go to the toilet. He was just skin and bones; his body totally wasted with cancer. He couldn't even get out of bed on his own. Yet he insisted on using the commode instead of a bedpan. His tall, lean companion lifted him round the waist and shoulders and crossed the bare wooden floor: there were no carpets. On the way back to his bed the old man suddenly stiffened and would have collapsed but for the arms holding him up. He was in great pain: something serious had happened. The tall man made him as comfortable as possible and set off down the road to find a telephone.

'Is that Petersfield Hospital?'

'I'm speaking from Liss. I have a friend who I think is about to die. He was discharged from your hospital some time ago. He has cancer. What should I do?'

The hospital voice began telling him how to ascertain when death had occurred.

'I want to know what to do now – while he's still alive... What do you mean, "there is nothing I can do?" Can't you send a doctor?'

'No.' The voice went on with details of how to ensure death had occurred, and how after a three-hour interval, to lay out the body – with a clean pair of pyjamas on it. 'A doctor will come later to certify death has occurred.'

When he got back to the bare bedroom all was quiet. At first he thought the old man had already died. No. His chest was moving up and down. He was dozing. Out of the blue the dozing man turned to his companion who was sitting in a wooden chair beside the bed.

'Len,' he said, 'I am dying, aren't I?'

There was a long pause. There was a gulp in Len's throat. Slowly he nodded.

The old man seemed to doze off again. But not for long. He turned to Len and blurted out the question: 'Do you believe in God?'

'God?' Len replied, surprised by the suddenness and the nature of the question. 'God?' he repeated. Then he replied, 'Yes, I do.'

There was another long pause.

'I used to be a Roman Catholic,' the old man volunteered. 'But that was a long time ago.'

He seemed to doze off for some minutes. As suddenly as he had asked the first question he said, 'Do you think you could call a priest for me?'

No such luxuries as a car, or even a bicycle in this house. Group-Captain Leonard Cheshire, VC, DSO, DFC, put on a jacket and went out into the Hampshire countryside in search of a Catholic priest.

The first few people he questioned did not know if there was a Catholic church in the town. Finally, a young girl of about ten pointed him in a direction where she thought there was a church. In due course Cheshire found the church and the priest. Father Clarke said he would come as soon as he could.

Meanwhile Cheshire returned to the house. He sat beside the dying man's bed. All he had to offer was his time. And his time, really, was the best gift he could offer. The smell was awful. The old man's cancer had spread to his liver, with the result he had little control of his bowels. Cheshire went out to get a basin of cold water. There was no hot water at all in the house. He then began the revolting task of cleaning the old man, trying hard to keep his nausea in check. He wondered when the priest would come. He couldn't find much to talk about to the old man. He began reading the book he had found on Father Clarke's table and which the priest had said he could borrow. It was 'One Lord, One Faith', an account by Monsignor Vernon Johnson of why, as a distinguished and popular Anglican clergyman, he had decided to become a Roman Catholic.

At seven o'clock in the evening Father Clarke arrived. He had been able to find the large, rambling house, Le Court, despite the greenery growing wild over the name plate. He had struggled with some difficulty to negotiate his little Austin car around the many pot-holes that dotted the long drive-way up to the house. The lawns and gardens had not been tended for months, maybe years.

The tall man led the priest, dressed in black, up the stairs to a bedroom on the first floor. There was no sign of any furniture or furnishings: no carpets, no curtains, no pictures, nothing. Just a bare bed.

There was no electricity in the house. Cheshire lit an oil-lamp. He watched as Father Clarke took out a small phial of oil. He couldn't fully understand what the priest seemed to be mumbling. Now and again his Merton College Latin helped him to pick out a few words. The priest anointed the old man's body. He gave him the *Viaticum*.

They left Arthur to doze.

'Would you like a cup of tea before you set out, Father?' Cheshire asked the priest.

Father Clarke was intrigued. A large country-house, dilapidated, left to rot. Was the man who was offering him tea a criminal on the run, 'squatting' where he could find shelter for the night?

'Thank you, yes,' he replied, repressing his first inclination which was to get back to his parish. He followed Cheshire into the kitchen. 'That old man upstairs,' he began, 'He's very ill. He should be in hospital, with proper medical attention.'

'You're dead right, Father. That's where he should be.' He paused as he searched for a tea-bag. 'He *was* in hospital. Then they found his illness was incurable. He was taking up a bed that could be used by someone who was not dying. They told him he must go home.'

Cheshire passed the priest a cup.

'But he had no home. So I took him in.'

'You're a doctor, I take it?' the priest presumed.

'No, I have no medical qualifications whatever.'

'Then how do you treat him?'

'I don't,' Cheshire replied. 'I have no medicines at all. I just look after him. What else could one do? Leave him to die on the streets?'

After the War Cheshire had felt an urge to work for a world in which peace would be a reality, but the dreams of doing this had not materialized. He embarked on a community scheme to help ex-servicemen resettle into civilian life, but that had failed, too, leaving him with a large empty house and a huge pile of debts. It was while he was selling off the estate to pay the creditors that he was asked by the local hospital if he could find alternative accommodation for one of the former members of the community scheme who was dying of cancer. That was how the old man was there.

Cheshire and the priest shook hands and parted. Cheshire tip-toed up the creaking stairs. The old man was sleeping. He sat by the bed. Inevitably his mind turned to the mushroom cloud over Nagaskai. He thought a lot about Nagaskai. How could he ever forget? The red and black billowing clouds, the flat white mushroom top, were to haunt him forever. Like the rest of the world, he could at least salve his conscience by saying that the necessary evil that had been done had at least staved a much larger evil. By forestalling the invasion of Japan some half a million American lives had been saved and at the same time several million Japanese lives, including men and women and children, had been saved. But then how many human victims must be sacrificially killed in order to avert a bigger calamity? Are we not then back in a pagan world of human sacrifice as a means of placating some superior power? What was the answer to it all? Was there an answer? It seemed that the West and the Soviet Union were even then hell-bent on a collision course of mutual annihilation. He picked up his book and began reading by the oil-lamp. Occasionally he would look across at the regular movement of the blanket moving up and down. Three hours later, Cheshire looked up from his book. Arthur Dykes was dead.

A few days later, apart from Father Clarke, Cheshire was the only person at Arthur's interment. He returned the book he had borrowed to the priest. He surprised him by then asking to be received into the Catholic Church. Cheshire believed in a God. An experience that he had had during the War had convinced him. He was at the Vanity Fair, a war-time bar off Piccadilly, drinking with his younger brother Christopher who had recently been repatriated after four years as a prisoner-of-war in Stalag Luft III.

Surprisingly, the conversation turned to religion. Cheshire thought this most inappropriate for his last night in London. With a view to ending it he said, 'God is an inward conscience, personal to each of us, that tells us what we ought to do and what we ought not; one thing to some of us, another to others. If only people wouldn't confuse the issue by bringing religion into it, the world would be a lot better off.'

'Absolute nonsense,' someone answered with considerable feeling. 'God is a person and you know it perfectly well. You ought to be ashamed of yourself.'

The bar went silent. Cheshire didn't want a fight. So he kept his silence, too. But he later recorded in a book what happened next. 'No sooner was that statement made than I knew it to be true. What until then had seemed nonsense now carried total conviction ... It all happened in a flash.'

On Christmas Eve 1948 Cheshire was received into the Catholic Church by Father Clarke.

Barely had they removed Arthur Dykes' body than a porter of a block of flats in London in which Cheshire's aunt lived called to see him. His grandmother-in-law, a lady of ninety-one, was living in a fifth-storey flat, unable to get out of bed and with only the district nurse to look after her. Would Cheshire take her in, as he had taken in Arthur?

The family house Cheshire lived in, 'Le Court', was derelict. Apart from his pension he had no funds to furnish it, even to buy sheets and blankets and mattresses. But what could he say?

Granny was followed by a cockney upholsterer from Hackney, Alf Wilmot, who was very ill and had nowhere to live. His persistent dry cough betrayed even to untrained ears the symptoms of advanced tuberculosis.

The waiting lists for available beds in hospitals were becoming so long and the needs so urgent that any patient who could no longer benefit from treatment had to be removed elsewhere. More TB patients followed. The proper disposal of sputum from the TB patients raised a major problem. Not surprisingly Cheshire himself contracted TB and later spent two and a half years in a sanatorium in Midhurst.

Johnny Moore was only sixteen when he came. Just after his fourteenth birthday he contracted transverse myoletis, a rare disease, which paralysed him from the waist down. He was put into a hospital with dying old men, until Cheshire rescued him. Cheshire would carry him up and down the stairs on his back.

Looking after all these people was beyond the capability of just one person. So the not-so-sick and not-so-disabled learned to look after those more ill and more disabled than they. Even Granny, aged ninety-one, would peel a bucket of potatoes each morning in her room. It was a red letter day when a trained nurse arrived, prepared to work for just pocket money. In the course of time Le Court was gradually transformed from a sort of doss house into a real home, where human wrecks, discarded by society, were able to regain their self-respect. This was the beginning of the Leonard Cheshire Homes.

In due course the first Home was followed by others in Britain and later all over the world. In 1981, there were 195 Homes in over forty countries, caring for 5000 people. In 1992 there were more than 270 Homes in Britain and in fifty countries abroad. The Homes offer care and shelter in an atmosphere as close as possible to that of a family. The majority of Homes cater for younger adult disabled persons, but there are also specialized Homes for disabled children, the mentally handicapped, burnt-out leprosy sufferers, and the old and infirm. The aim is to help each person achieve maximum independence.

In 1959 Cheshire married Sue Ryder, famous for her work in Poland among the survivors of the concentration camps after the war. They set up a joint mission, The Ryder-Cheshire Mission, for the relief of suffering, especially in the Developing World. There are Missions in India, Nepal, Tanzania, Australia and New Zealand, to cater for sufferers from tuberculosis, leprosy and mental handicaps.

In 1991 Cheshire was made a Life Peer and also Knight Grand Commander of the Order of Saint Gregory the Great.

Chapter Fourteen

Men for Others

While Sister Dominique and Father Takakura and their companions and colleagues were devoting their lives to the poor and needy in Japan, Father Arrupe was also embarked on a life of caring for the poor and the oppressed and those 'without a voice', not only in Japan, but also throughout the world.

In 1954, on the Feast of Saint Francis Xavier, Arrupe was summoned to Tokyo to be told that he would no longer be Novice Master at Nagatsuka: he was to be the Vice-Provincial of the Jesuit Order in Japan. He was now the Very Reverend Father Arrupe, although to his friends he always remained 'Don Pedro' or 'Perico'.

He invited Jesuits from all over the world to Japan. Under his guidance Sophia University, the Catholic University of Tokyo, added to its School of Arts and Economics, Colleges of Theology, Law, Foreign Languages, Foreign Affairs, Science and Technology, thus making it one of the leading private universities in Japan. It expanded greatly from 1500 students in 1945 to 6000 in 1986. In 1958 Japan was raised to a full Jesuit province and Arrupe was made the Society's first provincial superior in the country.

By now Arrupe had established himself as a wide-ranging thinker and prolific writer. He was the author of eight books in Japanese, including a life of St Francis Xavier, a five-volume commentary on the Spiritual Exercises of Ignatius Loyola and a translation of the works of St John of the Cross. He had also written (in Spanish) about Japan and the experience of the atomic bomb.

In October 1964 Father Janssens, the Superior General of the Jesuit Order, died. A Thirty-First General Congregation was called for May 1965 to elect a successor to lead the 36 000 Jesuits in the world. All the superiors of the several world provinces were summoned to Rome. Before the election of the General Father Maurice Giuliani of France exhorted the assembled Fathers, 'We need a General who will assist us, as companions of Jesus, to embrace the entire world in all its fullness and to co-operate in the redemption of our age.' Pope Paul VI called on the Society 'to employ its energies against one of the most serious maladies of the modern world, the widespread denial, in one form or another, of Almighty God.'

The Society of Jesus is a group of men called to be companions with Christ in his redeeming mission. Through four centuries men of excellence and high competence had made the energetic service of the Lord the characteristic of their spirituality whether it be composing astronomical tables at the Imperial Court of Peking, paddling down the St Lawrence River, lecturing on philosophy and theology at the Gregorian University in Rome, dying on the gallows at Tyburn, Marble Arch, adopting the role of *sanyassi* in India, developing communities of Amerindians in Paraguay, or giving their lives in the service of the plague-stricken in Andalusia. Ever open to diverse cultures of the world, ever ready to accommodate to constantly shifting situations, ever their objective was *Ad majorem Dei gloriam* (to the greater glory of God). Jesuits have also worked as masons, metallurgists, architects; they have laboured as farmers with the purpose of making life more humane for others; working with all men in constructing a better world.

The 224 delegates deliberated for two weeks. Finally, after two weeks, on the third ballot, they chose the superior general of the province of Japan, the *higaisha*, the survivor of the Hiroshima atom bomb, the Basque Pedro Arrupe to be the twenty-eighth Superior General of the Order, the twenty-seventh successor of St Ignatius Loyola.

Arrupe's Generalship, not surprisingly, was characterized by his concern for the poor, and by the demands of justice. Up to this time about one-third of all Jesuits were occupied in education, ranging from universities to secondary schools and primary schools for the poor. In most countries Jesuits became more conscious of their obligation to open their schools to young people of all classes. In April 1966 Arrupe wrote to the provincial of the Mexican province:

> Education, like all our ministries, should be studied and planned in terms of social problems. Certain colleges – because of their almost exclusive type of student or because of higher fees – raise serious doubts about their right to survive.

Four years later, to the dismay of many, Provincial Arrupe closed the Society's prestigious Instituto Patria for upper-middle-class high school boys and reopened it for poor and destitute students. The Jesuit College in Rio de Janeiro was transformed overnight when its doors were thrown open to the children of poor and moderate-income families, who attended the school in three shifts.

In an Address of July 1973, entitled 'Men for Others', Arrupe described the formation of 'men for others' as one of the chief objectives in the Society's educational work, an objective arising from:

[the] new awareness in the Church that participation in the promotion of justice and the liberation of the oppressed is a constitutive element of the mission which our Lord has entrusted to her.

The 1950s and 1960s had been the era of national liberation: country after country in Africa and Asia gained independence; more and more posts of importance were handed over to Africans and Asians. At the Thirty-Second General Congregation that Arrupe called in 1974, more than half of the 236 delegates were under fifty, nine under forty, and there were many non-white faces.

Arrupe's outstanding achievement was to commit this General Congregation to the defence of the poor and the under-privileged as a primary apostate. As he said, 'For hundreds of millions the real crisis of faith comes not from materialism nor from unrestricted theological discussion, but from the brutal misery of their own existence.' In one of its conclusions the Congregation records its awareness of:

millions of men and women in our world ... who are suffering from poverty and hunger, from the unjust distribution of wealth and resources and from the consequences of racial, social and political discrimination ... [and] those millions are hungry, not just for bread, but for the Word of God.

The Congregation passed a Decree that it called 'Our Mission Today', its central thrust being that

for us, the promotion of justice ... should be the concern of our whole life and a dimension of all our apostolic endeavours ... The best way to bring the Good News of God's love to man was by showing that his love makes us love man more. But since there can be no love without justice, action for justice is the acid test of our preaching of the Gospel.

It also recognized that

'Jesuits will be unable to hear the "cry of the poor" unless they have greater personal experience of the miseries and distress of the poor.'

Any suggestions of middle-class living were to be frowned upon. A more herioc poverty became the order of the day.

The Jesuits were soon in the forefront of what became known as 'liberation theology'. Arrupe supported the South American Jesuits in their efforts for the rural and urban workers against oppressive regimes, as in El Salvador. All this involved political involvement. In course of time many Jesuits were called on to give their lives in the service of the poor and the oppressed. In April 1975, just one month after the closure of the Thirty-Second General Congregation, North Vietnamese troops entered Saigon, leading to the break-up of the Jesuit mission of 69 men, most of whom were young Vietnamese priests and scholastics. Within six months in 1977/8 five Jesuits were murdered as they carried out their pastoral duties, one in Brazil, one in El Salvador, three in Zimbabwe. In 1981 a sixth was gunned down in the Philippines. In 1980 120 Chinese Jesuits, many old men, still remained in prison under sentence of twenty or more years. And still today the call is made for justice and still Jesuits respond with their lives.

This urgency which drives the Society in its solicitude for the poor and the underprivileged is not new – it is the same which drove the society in its very beginning. A decree of 1550 states that:

> The Society should show itself no less useful in reconciling the alienated or estranged, in serving those in hospitals and prisons and indeed in performing any work of love or charity as will seem to be for the glory of God and for the common good.

Father Arrupe travelled a great deal. He had to, if he was to keep in close touch with those thousands of Jesuits to whom he was the representative of St Ignatius himself. The fact that he could speak Spanish, English, French, German, Italian, Japanese and Latin, made communication easy and meaningful.

One experience moved him particularly.

A few years ago I was visiting one of the Jesuit provinces in Latin America. I was invited to celebrate Mass in a local neighbourhood, in a slum (*favela*) which was the poorest in the region, they tell me. About five thousand people were living there in the mud because this district was located in a low-lying area which flooded every time it rained.

I gladly accepted because I knew from experience that we learn much when we visit the poor. We do a great deal of good for the poor, but they, on their part, teach us many things.

The Mass was held in a small open building which was in a very poor state of repair; there was no door, and the dogs and cats came in and went out freely. Mass began with hymns accompanied by a self-taught guitarist, and the result was marvellous. The words of the hymn went: 'Loving is giving of oneself, forgetting oneself, while seeking what will make others happy'; and then it continued: 'How beautiful it is to live in order to love, how great it is to have in order to give. Giving joy and happiness, giving of oneself – this is love! If you love as you love yourself, and if you give yourself for others, you will see that there is no selfishness impossible to overcome. How beautiful it is to live in order to love.'

Progressively as the hymn continued I felt the lump in my throat. I had to make a real effort to continue the Mass. These people seemed to possess nothing and yet they were ready to give of themselves to communicate joy and happiness.

At the consecration I elevated the Host and perceived in the absolute silence the joy of the Lord which is found among those who love him. As Jesus said, 'He sent me to bring the good news to the poor,' (Luke 4:18). 'Happy are the poor in spirit,' (Matt 5:3).

A bit later, while distributing Communion, I noticed big tears like pearls on many of these faces, which were dry, hard, baked by the sun: they recognized Jesus, who was their only consolation. My hands were trembling.

My homily was short. It was more of a dialogue; they told me things that one rarely hears in solemn discourses, very simple things, but at the same time profound and touchingly sublime. A little old woman said, 'You are the Superior of the Fathers, aren't you? Well, sir, a thousand thanks, because your Jesuit priests brought us the great treasure we were lacking, what we needed most, Holy Mass.' A young boy stated publicly, 'Father, be assured that we are very grateful because the priests have taught us to love our enemies. A week ago I got out a knife to kill a guy whom I hated. But after listening to the priest explain the Gospel to us, I went out and bought an ice cream and gave it to my enemy.'

When it was over, a big devil whose hang-dog look made me almost afraid said, 'Come to my place. I have something to give you.' I was undecided, I didn't know whether to accept or not, but the priest who was with me said, 'Accept, Father, they are good people.' I went to his place; his house was a hovel nearly on the point of collapsing. He had me sit down on a rickety old chair. From there I could see the sunset. The big man said to me, 'Look, sir, how beautiful it is!' We sat in silence for several minutes. The sun disappeared. The man then said, 'I didn't know how to thank you for all you have done for us. I have nothing to give you, but I thought you would like to see this sunset. You liked it, didn't you? Good evening,' and then he shook my hand.

As I was leaving, I thought, 'I have met very few hearts that are so kind.*

Arrupe made several visits to Britain. On one of these he was making his way to the Jesuit Church in Farm Street, in Mayfair, London. He got out of the tube station at Marble Arch. He stopped at the Tyburn Way, in the middle of Marble Arch, where several English martyrs, including many Jesuits, had been hung, drawn and quartered. At Speakers' Corner someone was haranguing a small but lively crowd about some obviously important issue. But he couldn't stop; he was due to say the evening Mass.

He made his way up Park Lane. People were just beginning to vacate their deck chairs in the Park. At Mount Street he turned left, into Mayfair. At the same time another man had alighted from a Number 73 bus. He, too, headed into Mayfair. The slightly-stooping Basque was first to reach the Church. He stopped at a painting in the front of the church. It was a painting of St Francis Xavier, exhausted and dying, looking out to China where he was hoping to emulate the missionary work he had done in Japan. He stood in front of the painting for several minutes. He moved up the aisle and disappeared into the sacristy. Then, the tall, still erect, man arrived. He, too, stopped in front of the painting and stared at it for several minutes. If William Skardon, the M15 agent who had tracked down Klaus Fuchs, the atom bomb spy, was shadowing the activities of the two men, he would surely have concluded that the painting was a 'dropping' point, where state secrets were exchanged. Otherwise, why would they both spend so long there? But Mr Skardon was not there. And the two men had no state secrets to pass on. It was just that both of them had a great devotion to the subject of the painting.

The congregation stood as the priest – a smallish man, with a slight stoop, walked slowly to the main altar. He wore a heavily braided chasuble. The chasuble was red, the colour of blood. It was the feast day of a martyr. Slowly Father Arrupe climbed the few steps. He turned to face the people.

How appropriate, thought Cheshire, that he should be saying a Mass for a martyr. If anyone, he would know of martyrs. Yes, one quarter of a million of them, men, women, children, even babies. In fact, by all the laws of nature, he should have been one of them himself.

---

* Arrupe, Pedro, SJ, *One Jesuit's Spiritual Journey.*

And it was I, albeit indirectly, who participated in that slaughter. Because of me he should be dead. And yet he had done me no harm. I didn't even know him. He was not even my enemy. He was a Spaniard, from a small impoverished country. To all intents and purposes he was neutral. He had no right to die. But neither did the thousands of innocent men and women and children. They had done neither me nor anyone else any harm. But they had been put to the sword. The military. That was different. They lived by and for war. Death in battle was part of their profession. But how, in total war, could you separate the innocent and undeserving of death from the less innocent and more deserving? The Church was right. The Second Vatican Council had decreed that war that tends indiscriminately to destroy entire cities and large areas with their inhabitants was a crime against God and humanity and merited unhesitating and unequivocal condemnation. A nuclear war was very difficult to justify. Even for the best of ends it is not permitted to do evil. Total war – destruction of cities and civilian populations – is nothing but mass murder.

He thought back to that morning, many years ago, as he looked out of *Bock's Car* on Nagasaki. At that time neither the Church nor anyone else knew of any weapon that could produce such massive destruction.

The bombs on Hiroshima and Nagasaki had eliminated any lingering notion of a 'just' war. The weapons and strategies of modern warfare, not only nuclear, but also bacteriological and chemical, could not be accommodated to the traditional concept of a 'just' conflict. For many, like the Quakers, any war is a total violation of humanity, immoral and unjust. In 1943 Franz Jaegerstaether, an ordinary peasant, was publicly beheaded in his village for refusing to serve in Hitler's army. He was a hero – because of his conscience. The cowards are those who surrender their moral judgement. At that very time, in the United States, Daniel Berrigan, like the celebrant of the Mass, a Jesuit, was in prison for his conscientious objection to the Vietnam war. Non-violence (civil disobedience) was the means of defence used by men such as Mahatma Gandhi, by the insurgents of Prague in August 1968, by the Jews in the USSR, by black civil rights leaders in the USA.

The priest was washing his hands. In profile you could make out his typical slightly hooked, Basque nose. He faced the congregation, his arms extended.

'Pray, brethren, that our sacrifice may be acceptable to God, the almighty Father.'

Their eyes met. One had observed the most powerful weapon of destruction ever contrived by the genius of man wreak its indiscriminate annihilation. The other had stood, silent, unsuspecting, a lamb to the slaughter. By some mysterious quirk of fate the priest was alive; by an equally mysterious quirk millions were not. He was their spokesperson.

'May the merits and prayers of your martyrs gain us your constant help and protection.'

Again their eyes met.

'Dying you destroyed our death, rising you restored our life. Lord Jesus, come in glory.'

The Mass continued.

'Remember, Lord, those who have died and have gone before us. For ourselves, too, we ask some share in the fellowship of your apostles and martyrs. Though we are sinners we trust in your mercy and love. Do not consider what we truly deserve, but grant us your forgiveness.'

The tinkle of a bell warned of the coming consecration of the bread and wine. With the rest of the congregation Cheshire went on his knees.

He looked up. He fought hard to control his emotions. Below was desolation and carnage, out of which billowed ugly black and red clouds, angrily jostling each other out of the way; the clouds rose until they reached a pinnacle, fanning out into a white mushroom; and above the mushroom a white Host, lifted aloft by this priest and a whole multitude of humanity clinging to his vestments. By now Cheshire was shaking. He lowered his gaze. He buried his head in his hands.

He rose with the congregation.

'Deliver us, Lord, from every evil, and grant us peace in our day.'

His eyes were misted. So he couldn't see whether the eyes of the priest were also misted. Perhaps they were.

Father Arrupe began the prayer for peace and unity. 'Lord Jesus Christ, you said to your apostles: I leave you peace, my peace I give you. Look not on our sins, but on the faith of your Church, and grant us the peace and unity of your kingdom where you live for ever and ever.'

The people began to shake hands, expressing their love for one another. Father Arrupe again caught the eye of the famous bomber pilot, the war hero. He smiled. Cheshire responded likewise. All was forgiven, then. There was peace and reconciliation between victor and vanquished, between the living few and the multitude dead.

The Mass moved to its close. Father Arrupe moved his right hand across the assembled throng, from left to right. 'May the blessing of Almighty God come upon you and remain with you forever.'

The Group Captain, VC, bowed his head. All was peace. He said his own special prayer, published in his book *The Light of Many Suns*. 'My prayer is that the immense forces hidden in seemingly inert matter will ever remind us of the far higher order of power in the spirit of man, the power of love.'

After the blessing, the priest took hold of the veil covering the chalice and paten and went into the sacristy. The congregation began to move out. Soon there were just a few old women left and perhaps two tramps – over-devout or keeping out of the cold.

Cheshire walked up the side aisle and knocked gently on the sacristy door. A well-groomed, moustachioed, man, equally tall and erect, with a very military bearing, answered the knock. He had a frown on his face, obviously expecting the usual down-and-out begging for alms from the priest. After all, this was no ordinary priest. But the man who had knocked was obviously not a down-and-out.

'Could I have a word with the priest?' he inquired.

'Is it anything special?'

'Nothing unduly special.'

'What is it then?' The ex-military man wanted to save the time of Father Arrupe.

'We have something in common.'

The other man wondered what the two could have in common.

'Just say "Pika-Don".'

'Pika-Don?' He frowned even more deeply. 'Pika-Don? What on earth is that?' he asked somewhat impatiently.

Cheshire was about to say 'You wouldn't understand'; but he thought that was being unduly uncharitable. 'The priest will understand,' he said instead.

The man came back.

'He'll be with you in a few minutes.'

Cheshire returned to his seat in the pew. The old women – and the tramps – were still there. Presently the priest came up to him. They didn't speak. They knew each other from reputation. Yes, they certainly did have Pika-don in common. One had been at the receiving end; the other had been at the delivering end.

They both genuflected before the Blessed Sacrament and made their way out. If Luis Alvarez – who had initiated Cheshire into the mysteries of the Thin Man and the Fat Man on the tiny Pacific island of Tinian – had been there to see the two walking along together he would have named them the 'long man' and the 'short man'.

It was now dusk and decidedly cold. The Spaniard pulled his scarf closely about his neck. 'You said we have one thing in common,' he said. 'Pika-Don, yes,' he went on.

Cheshire nodded.

'In fact we have two big things in common,' the priest said, a smile breaking round his mouth, his two fingers raised to make the point.

'Two?' Cheshire wondered.

Arrupe looked up at the puzzled expression. 'Two, Yes.' Then, almost in a whisper. 'Faith.'

'Of course,' Cheshire thought to himself. 'Yes,' he replied after a pause, 'Yes, I suppose that about sums it all up.'

The two 'men for others' strode off. They never met again.

POSTSCRIPT

On 7 August 1981, thirty-five years and one day after the atom bomb on Hiroshima, Father Arrupe was returning from a visit to the Philippines on the occasion of the 400th anniversary of the arrival of the Jesuits there. He was struck down by a stroke due to cerebral thrombosis. He was left much debilitated. The 'voice of those who had no voice' could no longer speak. His health declined. In September 1983 he resigned as the twenty-seventh successor of Saint Ignatius. He had led the Jesuits through one of the most sensitive periods of their history in the wake of the Second Vatican Council. On 5 February 1991, aged 83, the little big man, so unshakeably certain of the essential truths of his faith as not to be fussed by accidentals and passing anxieties such as atom bombs, died in Rome.

Not quite a year later, on 31 July 1992, Group Captain – now Lord – Cheshire, VC, OM, who had won the country's two highest honours – for valour in 1944 and for merit in 1981, also died.

At the close of the Thirty-Fourth General Congregation of the Jesuits held in Rome in March 1995 it was revealed that moves would begin in 1996 for the beatification of Father Arrupe because of his personal sanctity and his inspirational commitment to the plight of refugees and the poor. (Beatification is the first step in the process of canonization, the formal declaration of a saint, and can only begin five years after a person's death.) There was a demand, too, that his body be brought back from Verano cemetery and be interred in the Church of the Gésu in Rome, where the remains of St Ignatius of Loyala and St Francis Xavier lie.

BIBLIOGRAPHY

Arrupe, Pedro SJ, *One Jesuit's Spiritual Journey*. (Autobiographical Conversations with Jean-Claude Dietsch, SJ), The Institute of Jesuit Sources, St Louis, Missouri, 1986.

Arrupe, Pedro SJ, 'Surviving the Atomic Bomb', In *Recollections and Reflections of Pedro Arrupe, SJ*, Michael Glazier, Wilmington, Delaware, USA 1986 (Originally published Mexico, 1965)

Arrupe, Pedro SJ, *A Planet to Heal*. International Centre for Jesuit Education, Rome, Italy, 1977.

Cheshire, Leonard, *The Hidden World*. Collins, London, 1981. *The Light of Many Suns*, Methuen London, 1985

Costello, John, *The Pacific War*, Collins, London, 1981.

Glynn, Paul, *A Song for Nagasaki*, Collins, London, 1990.

Hersey, John, *Hiroshima*, Penguin, London, 1946.

Hirschfield, Burt, *A Cloud over Hiroshima*, Bailey Brothers and Swinfen Ltd, Folkestone, 1974.

Hoover, J. Edgar, *The Crime of the Century: The Case of the A-Bomb Spies*, The Reader's Digest, London, June 1951.

Jungk, Robert, *Brighter Than A Thousand Suns*, Penguin, London, 1958. *Children of the Ashes*, Heinemann, London, 1959.

Moorehead, Alan, *The Traitors*, Hamish Hamilton Ltd., London, 1952.

O'Callaghan, Joseph T., SJ, *I was Chaplain on the Franklin*, The MacMillan Co., New York, 1961.

O'Malley, William J., SJ, *The Fifth Week*, Loyola University Press, Chicago, 1976.

Osada, Arata, *Children of the A-Bomb*, Peter Owen, London, 1963.

Searles, Hank, *Kataki*, Robert Hale, London, 1987.

Also personal communications from:

Father Franz Miltrup, SM, Latten, Germany.
Father Adam Müller (A Biographical Note, Translated by Fr Miltrup).
Father Paul Pfister, SJ, Jesuit House, Tokyo, Japan.

Other books by George Bishop

Teaching Mathematics in the Secondary School and
Teaching Mathematics in the Primary School (Collins, Glasgow 1963)
Experimental Science for Tropical Science, 3 vols (Collins, Glasgow 1963)
Curriculum Development, A textbook for students (Macmillan, 1985)
Innovation in Education (Macmillan, 1986)
Alternative Strategies in Education (Macmillan, 1989)
Travels in Imperial China, The Exploration and Discoveries of Père David (Cassell, 1990)
Eight Hundred Years of Physics Teaching (Fisher Miller Publishing, 1994)
The Hibiscus Years (Fisher Miller Publishing, 1995)

Fisher Miller Publishing provides a service for authors. We arrange editing, typesetting, printing or a complete self-publishing package, at cost but to professional standards, tailored to your requirements and your pocket. We specialise in short print runs and books which mainstream publishers find uneconomic to publish. You, the author, keep control, and you receive the profits. If you are interested in our services, please contact us at Wits End, 11 Ramsholt Close, North Waltham, Hants RG25 2DG (tel/fax 01256 397482).